To Che Harris

From

Tom & M.B.

with

Lots of Love

16-

ALSO BY NANCY WOOD

Fiction

The Last Five Dollar Baby
The King of Liberty Bend
The Man Who Gave Thunder to the Earth

Poetry

Hollering Sun
Many Winters
War Cry on a Prayer Feather

Nonfiction

Colorado: Big Mountain Country
Clearcut: The Deforestation of America
The Grass Roots People
When Buffalo Free the Mountains

Photography

In This Proud Land (with Roy Stryker)
Heartland New Mexico: The Photographs of the
    Farm Security Administration, 1935–43

TAOS PUEBLO

TAOS
PUEBLO

by Nancy Wood

With an Introduction by Vine Deloria, Jr.

Alfred A. Knopf   New York   1989

Isabel Archuleta.

For Ben Marcus—Red Willow Dancing

THIS IS A BORZOI BOOK PUBLISHED BY ALFRED A. KNOPF, INC.

Copyright © 1989 by Nancy Wood

Introduction copyright © 1989 by Alfred A. Knopf, Inc.

All rights reserved under International and Pan-American Copyright
Conventions. Published in the United States by Alfred A. Knopf, Inc., New York,
and simultaneously in Canada by Random House of Canada Limited, Toronto.
Distributed by Random House, Inc., New York.

Library of Congress Cataloging-in-Publication Data

Wood, Nancy C.
  Taos pueblo.

  Bibliography: p.
  1. Taos Pueblo (N.M.)—Pictorial works 2. Taos
Indians—Pictorial works. 3. Indians of North America—
New Mexico—Pictorial works. I. Title.
E99.T2W62 1989   978.9'53   88-45785
ISBN 0-394-56032-9

Manufactured in the United States of America

First Edition

Above all is the long-living spirit
Which is the thread from generation to generation,
As long as the land we live on is everlasting,
And our children have a place to lie down.

Contents

Overleaf: View from the south side of the pueblo, c. 1884.
(William Henry Jackson, Colorado Historical Society)

Introduction

Success in the modern world seems to involve creating a gap in credibility between what something is and what you would like it to be and selling this difference to a gullible public that begs to be conned out of its socks. Since American Indians are not a familiar item with people in the large cities or on the coasts, it is not difficult to construct a fantasy world of buckskin and peddle it to the first greedy or unsuspecting publisher looking to fill out his fall lists. The literature, if one can call it that, dealing with American Indians that now floods the market is stunning in that it generally describes a people and a world that never were, never will be, and probably should not be under any circumstances.

New Age literature in particular uses Indian images to promulgate a psychological and fictional world in which "power" becomes the dominant element of experience and the earthly, demanding, and disruptive practices of tribal religion become an instant vision of wholeness and love. Not only are the real Indians submerged beneath this conglomerate of cushy feelings and self-evident homilies, the non-Indian practitioners appropriate Indian ideas wholesale, place them in entirely inappropriate contexts, and proceed to expound on great truths which Aesop would have rejected as unworthy for his fables.

This book does not follow any of these formulas and, indeed, takes such a different approach that it is at first puzzling and then disturbing in a fundamental way. The book deals with the people of Taos Pueblo, a small Indian village located in northern New Mexico, one of the twenty or more Pueblos which have dominated the Rio Grande valley since time immemorial, at least during most of the time represented by human history, which is, for our purposes, time immemorial. It is an intensely personal book but also a book that has a dispassionate analysis and observation that is quite refreshing. The outstanding character of Nancy Wood's book is that it does and can move from personal reflection to astute observation and move quickly back to human emotion again without confusing the reader or losing the thread of the story.

Taos has long been admired, by Indian and non-Indian alike, as the citadel, the bastion, of traditional Indian religion. Non-Indian luminaries such as D.H. Lawrence, Mabel Dodge Luhan, and Carl Jung have helped to spin a web of fantasy and mystery around Taos, and during the postwar years several generations of young Americans have picked up this strand of worship and respect and woven it into a tapestry of wisdom and religious purity that is accepted without question by many people who will never visit Taos in their lives. So potent is this aura of religiosity and tradition that many visitors simply take it for granted that they have had a unique experience at Taos, and the Pueblo has thousands of visitors a year who leave the place firmly believing they have paid proper homage to one of the continent's prominent religious shrines.

Nancy Wood does not fall into this emotional trap and she gives us a rather unique look at rapid and radical change, continuing and enduring values, and a society in great stress and flux that is now transforming itself into something entirely different from anything anyone could have predicted. Her observations are firm, incisive, and pointed, sometimes expressing her own bewilderment, other times recounting her admiration and her affection, but always trying to find the fulcrum point of truth that will enable her to tell the real story of what is happening at Taos in a manner that will express the innate dignity of the people of the village. This concern will become more apparent if we place this book and its observations within the context of modern American Indian life and how it has radically and permanently changed during this century.

Moving to the reservations was very traumatic for Indians. The old days of freedom died very quickly for most tribes. Within a few years, often less time than it would have taken for a person to get a college degree, a whole people was driven from the vast area of their ancestral homes and placed on tiny barren tracts of land where they were forced to adopt new customs, new religions, and new ways of supporting themselves. The government was thorough. For many years even a gathering of Indians on the reservations was prohibited. Social ceremonies were submerged beneath secular American holidays, and domestic practices designed to keep families together were banned. Children were forcibly taken from their homes, moved to large cold institutional settings in the eastern United States, and forced to learn a new language and new social practices. Setting a table for afternoon tea replaced the knowledge of how to bake bread in an outdoor oven; reciting the presidents of the United States and the books of the Bible became more important than learning how to plant and hunt. Most important, the continuing relationship with the land and animals was reduced to a few hours of "recreation" set aside to make certain that the Indians had "good health."

Between 1870 and 1900 most of the western tribes had made this major adjustment and were beginning to prosper in their new lives. That is to say, as traumatic as the adjustment was, people had the capability to make changes and did so. The Indian societies that were so attractive to Carl Jung and John Collier, the New Deal Commissioner of Indian Affairs—the colorful figures who provided models for the Boy Scouts and other non-Indian "character-building" groups—were not the original pre-contact Indians. They were first generation reservation Indians, people who had carefully worked to accommodate themselves to the new world in which they were forced to live. They had accepted deliberate changes, but had not thrown over their culture and religion without a backward glance.

Most tribal religions required space—plenty of it—because the tribe had lived so long in a particular region and many of its memories had become attached to particular places and seasons, and both tribal history and religion were spread out over a vast area of land. In the Pacific Northwest the tribes followed the migratory patterns of the salmon, moving at least four times a year so that they would always be present when the rest of nature was making its seasonal changes. The Plains Indians followed the patterns of the buffalo, virtually herding them each year and maintaining a ceremonial year that paralleled quite closely the birth and death cycle of the game animals of the region. The settled peoples of the Southwest were sedentary quite early—remnants of their many settlements are scattered luxuriously over most of New Mexico and Arizona—so they developed their ceremonial year by dividing themselves into two groups, summer and winter people, and each group became responsible for participating in certain natural cycles which ensured growth and prosperity. Taos, in this respect, had one of the most sensible and complex ceremonial years.

Reduction to reservation status meant that certain ceremonies now became articles of faith, parts of the social and communal moral code, and admonitions passed along by elders and grandparents. They no longer were outward expressions of an inner reality. Many tribal religions shifted from actions to stories of how the people used to behave, and when this emphasis emerged it was almost certain that tribal life would itself begin to decline. Religion is primarily a way of acting; when it becomes a way of describing how we should believe—or what we should believe—it rapidly loses its potency and transforms itself into a history or a philosophy. It was this shift at Taos that made it so attractive to its early non-Indian visitors and gave Taos its prominence as a bastion of Indian traditions. Had Jung, Mabel Dodge Luhan, and D.H. Lawrence come across the people of Taos in the early 1700s, they would not have understood a single word or action. But by the 1920s much of the action had become oral commentary and even then people were bemoaning the fact of confinement and the deterioration of ceremonies and traditions.

The power of Taos and other strongholds of Indian life in the 1920s was sufficient to inspire a generation of non-Indians to see the substance of tribal society and to work for its preservation. In 1934, in a radical shift of emphasis directed primarily by John Collier, a great admirer of Taos, the federal government promoted the organization of Indian tribes into recognized and self-governing units which could direct the activities of the people on the reservations and rebuild tribal culture. Sympathetic as this program was, it was not the answer that Indians sought because it naively assumed that cultural traits could be preserved while adopting the practices of the white man. If Indians were now allowed to perform ancient dances which assisted in preserving the fertility of the land, they were also expected to welcome electricity and appliances into their homes and save toward furnaces, radios, and the rest of the things which make the modern homemaker delight in her leisure hours. Taos would have none of it, and battles raged for a generation over the degree to which the people should open their system of values, because they were plainly artificial ways of living. The results of the New Deal for Indians were further and even more rapid movement of religious ceremonials toward a system of beliefs and homilies.

The 1950s saw a radical shift toward assimilation under a policy called "termination," which sought rapid and often forced dissolution of tribal assets, primarily lands, and relocation of the reservation populations into urban America. The Pueblos escaped the worst of this policy because their outward ceremonial life had become such a tourist attraction that they were seen as a positive economic force in southwestern recreational economies. Termination did work to place their water rights, land titles, and hunting rights in increasing jeopardy but the public image of the humble, peaceful, and religious Pueblos stood them in good stead when

the policy-makers of Washington sought out tribes to experience this new direction.

As might be expected, the 1960s saw another complete reversal of federal policy. Instead of terminating the reservations, it was admitted that Indians would always be around and consequently policy was oriented toward educating the younger generation and bringing housing, jobs, and small businesses to the reservations. Indians became a favored minority in American society because they did not want to compete with the whites, they did not want to move into the cities, and they did not want to move next door and ruin property values in the suburbs. The problem of the 1960s was that once the government decided to assist Indians, it wanted to see instant and positive action on the reservations. Almost every grant was a pilot project of some kind, a minor investment of government time and money; the idea was that if the project proved successful, tribal funds or even foundation grants would be used to fund the activity on a continuing basis. A large capital debt began to hang over the heads of many tribes that accepted grants indiscriminately when the money was available, and only later understood what kind of a financial commitment they had made for the long term.

During the Reagan years the great benefits of unrestricted capitalism were preached by the government even while it was cutting out the important overhead monies which had previously kept the tribes afloat. If the tribes had been able to get a defense contract and sell claw hammers for $800 each, like some Reagan supporters, the policy might have worked. But the Indians were expected to begin at the bottom of the economic pyramid and work their way tediously up its many tiers to success. A breakthrough of sorts occurred when the Administration looked the other way and allowed the tribes to establish bingo halls to increase their annual income. This move placed Indians in competition with the American Legion, the Catholic Church, the VFW, and other private and religious groups who had been allowed to use one of man's basic sins to enhance their ability to do good works. The Reagan policy was accompanied by encouraging statements to the effect that Indians were just as good as anyone else and therefore could compete if given the chance, a message of hope totally foreign to the values of most Indian people.

The more traditional tribes—most prominently among them the Taos—rejected most of this rhetoric and tried to maintain a sense of continuity with the past. It was demeaning, many Indians felt, to have a culture and a religious tradition thousands of years old and to be holding nightly bingo games to preserve these things. But the onslaught of the modern world, combined with intensive and continuous change in the education of their children, placed most of the traditional groups in a state of great confusion and disarray. Too many things were happening too fast. The picture of Taos which Nancy Wood paints in this book is an accurate account of the trauma recently experienced by the people of this Pueblo. It is, in many ways, a distressing and disturbing situation but certainly not without precedent in Indian memories.

The various government efforts to manipulate Indian culture and history, and even Indian identity, beginning with the New Deal and Collier's idea of the red Atlantis, continuing through termination, self-determination, and Reaganesque capitalism, have produced some unexpected by-products which must be noted lest the reader see in the present difficulties at Taos the end of the trail for this group of Indians. By about 1936, when Indians had developed confidence that they could practice their religious ceremonies without immediate repression and reprisals from the government, the reservations began to see a revival of the old ways. It was not possible to move to the level of individual ceremonial life at that time because the economic conditions separated families, required long absences from the reservations, and forced substitutions in many of the ceremonial offices of the tribes. Nancy recounts in many of the stories of the people of Taos the long time that some of the elders had to remain away from the Pueblo in order to support themselves.

Religion and customs underwent two basic changes from 1936 to about 1968: More and more, the tradition appeared to be a philosophy of life rather than a way of life which involved particular actions, and much of the ceremonial life became the focus of tourist attractions. During the 1950s in particular, much of the tribal income that was available for the tribal government and for programs came from fees charged for taking pictures, posing for pictures, or for allowing people to attend ceremonies. Outward activities thus became social in the recreational sense and people experienced a vacuum in their own emotional lives. By the late 1960s the pressing question in Indian country concerned modern Indian identity. What did real Indians do? How did real Indians act? The question involved thinking through the stereotypical images of the Indian originating in the past and supported primarily by non-Indian expectations, and the new sense of cultural freedom generated by the ability of the younger generation to succeed, albeit most of the time temporarily, in the white man's world.

Indian activism accentuated the visible gap between what people felt and what society—and their peers—expected them to be. The more traditional groups such as Taos pulled themselves in with the hope of preserving some of the things of the past. But other tribes, which had been virtually obliterated by migrations away from the reservation, by acceptance of the non-Indian educational system, and by the attractions of the horn of plenty of modern American consumer society, had no place else to go to regain their identity except to one or two surviving elders or even the elders of other tribes. The drive to achieve a modern Indian identity was thus wholly familiar and at the same time wholly new. It provided a rational basis for doing things in that people could now make comparisons between the old ways and the white man's way based on their knowledge of the white man's way. This comparison had never been possible and once younger Indians saw the differences—and the reasons behind the old customs—they began to slip away from the belief that the white world offered the only alternative, and, in obscure places, interest in the traditions began to take on a life of its own.

In the last two decades there has been a new and amazing drive to bring the old ways to life and make them the substance of the new Indian societies. I first encountered this movement in northern Michigan in the mid-1970s when an old woman confided to me that the teenagers were being sent on vision quests in the woods once again.

During the Wounded Knee trials it became apparent to many young Sioux that the tribal language was a powerful political tool in the courtroom because non-Indians could not understand it. Benefits given to raise funds for legal defense began to feature Indian flute players, not country and western singers. Bilingual programs began to stress the native language and viewed English in many instances as *the* foreign language. Reservation leaders began to seek out traditional men and ask their advice on tribal political matters. In a recent conversation with a young Sioux politician I learned that within a few years it will be regarded as a natural, informal requirement that a man be a pipe carrier in order to run for tribal office. In short, Indian country is seeing an amazing revival of traditional forms, and these forms are manifest in the actions, not simply the words, of the people.

The conditions at Taos, described by Nancy Wood so vividly, now make sense in the context of historical developments among the many tribes of the continent. Taos, having been one of the traditional strongholds for so many years, is just now suffering the erosion and loss of faith that many other tribes experienced half a century ago. The trauma at Taos may eventually be more severe than that suffered by other tribes because it has been so faithful to its beliefs for so long a period of time. It is almost as if the Pueblo sits at the end of a massive whip that is cracking and re-forming its curve again. The hope that Nancy sees in the people of Taos may take another generation to fulfill itself but there is no question that it will come storming back in a blossoming of the old culture in a startlingly new form. That is evident in the many sketches of the people contained in the book, where the people express both dismay and hope, discouragement and reverence for the old ways.

In this situation an even more serious condition is evident. In the large sweep of history described in the oral traditions of the tribes is the prophecy that the planet undergoes certain "ages," in which certain things are featured and certain things endure. At the beginning of each age, "peoples" are created and they are given a specific mission with specific ceremonial requirements, certain rites and rituals, and specific predictions about the coming of

the end of the age. *The Book of the Hopi* contains some of these prophecies from the perspective of that tribe, and other books give sanitized versions of the beliefs of other tribes.

The primary requirement for the changing of an age is that the ceremonies wear out; people finally stop believing and abandon their old ways; people search for new ways and new messages. Since these ceremonies and rituals are designed for a specific age, they cannot be brought into the new age to come. Therefore a decline of the old ways is necessary for growth to new things. Like a fruit tree that blossoms, has its season, and goes into decline in order to produce new fruit the next season, so ceremonial life must vanish or become dormant if the people are to survive the catastrophes of the end of the age and emerge into the new age as a people ready to be re-formed. Ceremony is the creation of a special model of the creation using the wholly natural things that constitute a world: people, plants, animals, earth, water, and prayer. Substitution of portions of the ceremony—manufactured footwear for moccasins, processed tobacco for natural tobacco, plastic beads for bone and stone—all contribute to the gradual erosion of both the ceremony and the world which is now ending. The people must be faithful to the form throughout that particular world but even they realize that things are coming to an end.

The central element of Indian life is the family, and by this idea we mean the greatly extended family: all relatives by blood and law, all people adopted into the family network, and those very special plants, animals, birds, and other forms of life which have a particular relationship with that specific group of people. The non-Indian has a difficult time conceiving a family in these terms because of the long tradition of individualism and the more recent emphasis on the nuclear family in Protestant middle class thought. And the family is so familiar to Indians that most people feel it need not be explained. In the sketches of personal life here—the baking of bread, the knowledge of the grandfathers of when and how to plant corn, the memories of the animals and birds—are the family memories of the Taos people.

At the re-formation of life when a new age

begins, people and other life-forms adopt new relationships. Indeed, a great variety of new forms of life are produced. If people were to carry forward these relationships and this knowledge, they would be bringing into the new world outmoded ways of doing things. The new ways of doing things must be revealed to them when the new age starts. So the erosion of knowledge and decline of relationships is also a necessary part of life. The family is stripped to its basic core, which is that group of people that is deeply committed to each other and accepts responsibilities to provide for each other. When the new age begins this basic group is therefore expanded according to the principles of the new age. The bewilderment of the people of Taos at the disintegration of the family should be seen in this considerably broader context. The Pueblo is now experiencing a sorting-out of these intimate family relationships.

Indians, unfortunately, are no more able to predict the end of an age than are charismatic Christians or any other group that has an eschatological dimension to their religious beliefs. If you were to ask even the most knowledgeable and sophisticated medicine person about these things, they would give you an entirely honest answer: they really don't know. It always *seems* as if the world is coming to an end because the signs they have been told to look for are all appearing. But these signs have appeared before, especially during the times when the Spanish came, when the Mexicans came, and when the first Americans came. Life did fundamentally change but the people made adaptations and continued to live, sometimes briefly prospering before their conditions deteriorated again. Traditional Indians live in a strange kind of twilight where they have to be alert to changes but not excited by them. A deep hope and faith are integral to traditional existence.

So life in many Indian tribes is pretty much what Nancy Wood has depicted here: a tenuous balance of old and new, a deep sense of regret at the passage of time and change of conditions, but not yet a willingness to abandon the old teachings and jettison a group identity which has served them for countless centuries. But notice how often, in the recorded conversations of the younger people, we find a sense of wonder that goes back to the ancestors, and we marvel at the fact that countless generations have danced, laughed, and cried at these very adobe walls and plaza. Here we have not only a summing up of tribal existence but a reflection on the meaning of the present—again, the necessary mental attitude which points toward the ending of the age.

Through her many years of contact with the people of Taos, Nancy Wood has been able to look at the conditions at Taos without processing them through rose-colored glasses. She is able to experience the dreadful sadness of a way of life under severe pressure to change and she has recorded some of the change here. Many of the pictures show a deliberate juxtaposition of old and new, capturing a community in the process of change, discarding what is no longer useful, and taking whatever it can to replace the old. In the midst of this great confusion of images, she quite properly places the family at the center of concern. The family members become the spokespeople for what is happening at Taos, and through the confusion we see a determination to continue as a people.

Taos is, as Nancy correctly points out in the historical section, a strange mixture of Pueblo, mountain, and plains people, held together by ancient ceremony and legend and cemented into a unity by the place itself and the responsibilities of the summer and winter people. Its prolonged isolation from the modern world now makes it a prime candidate to suffer the onslaughts of modern life, and the primary question is one of intensity. To what degree will modern conditions erode the unity of Taos? And to what degree of cultural intensity will the inevitable rebounding extend? English may become the language of the kiva only temporarily, and then the ancient language will reassert itself and burst through the confines of the kiva into the Pueblo itself. Will Taos provide the priesthood for the new world? *That* question is very interesting and concerns not simply the people of Taos but other Indians and non-Indians as well.

The cardinal principle of Indian life in the old days was the truth. People could not afford to be misled when they had to be alert to the changes in nature, in life, and in the other peoples around them. Thus it was the most dreadful of all sins to lie, and more individuals were killed or banished for lying than suffered the same fates for killing a member of the tribe. Truth also gave testimony of respect. To lie, or even shade the truth, meant that the person had little respect for another, that he did not believe the other sufficiently mature to handle the truth. But there was a place for telling the truth. One did not needlessly or carelessly force an issue that might be deeply personal. Consequently, as many long-time observers of Indians will affirm, people simply sat quietly hoping that the people would themselves recognize the situation.

Writing a tough, honest book about Indians today is a difficult and sometimes even a hazardous task. There is great confusion in many tribes and the popular spokespeople of a tribe sometimes believe that if conditions are not mentioned, no one will notice them or, even worse, that the conditions themselves do not exist unless there is someone who thoughtlessly points them out. In many respects some Indians have adopted the concern for images which dominates American life and they regard any accurate rendering of the facts as harmful to the Indian cause. But the cause cannot be judged in the small time frame of the last century. Indeed, it must be seen in the context of hundreds of centuries and the experiences of the people over that period of time. When this larger context is provided, then the conditions we see at Taos become very interesting. They can be likened to the preliminary birth pains of a new community and they can be seen as definite signposts in the much larger canvas of Indian experiences in this age, now coming to an end.

Nancy Wood has paid the people of Taos a high compliment in her book. In telling the truth in a highly personal way she has accepted the humanity and the historical struggles of the people and sketched out the broader communal picture of life

today. She has shown that they have overcome past obstacles and are now in the midst of devising ways to overcome new difficulties. In a real sense this book helps to lift an artificial burden from the backs of the Taos people so that they can honestly say to their visitors: "We are an ordinary people trying to live in this world." And they can then mutter to themselves: "an ordinary people with an extraordinary responsibility to prepare ourselves for life in a new world that is coming."

This strange dualism, this mixture of confusion and confidence, has always made Taos special. Indians have always seen this strength at Taos when others saw only the colorful ceremonialism, the quaint personalities of the elders, and the seeming agelessness of the Pueblo itself. But even here there are two levels of confusion. One level is that of humility, the recognition that we are mortal and do make dreadful mistakes, that no divine plan, no prophecy, is ideally realized. The other level is honest bewilderment. Knowing that the people would have to overcome many obstacles in this world, did it really have to be *this*, an entirely onerous, practical, and unpleasant task seemingly unworthy of people who work with Father Sun and Mother Earth to ensure the continuance of life?

Questions give forth new questions, answers are superseded by new answers because life goes on. Consequently we see, demonstrated over and over again in this book, that living fully each day is the best and only way of resolving the riddles of existence. But it does help, deep within oneself, if there in the landscape are ruins of the old villages, the dust of generations past, who still give their testimony that they have brought life to us and brought us to this moment, and it is now our turn, however unprepared we might be, to continue and leave, as they did, a small trace that marks our passage through time to inspire those who come after us.

Preface

The first time I saw Taos Pueblo was on a brilliant March afternoon in 1961. I was not yet twenty-five years old, a refugee from the east, and an aspiring writer with two small children to support. At that time, I lived in Colorado Springs, a stuffy, conservative, military town where part of me remained incomplete. I yearned for spiritual and emotional renewal, for the kind of experience that would expand every fiber of my being. I had come to Taos, at the very beginning of the counter-culture movement, to try and find new roots, new meaning.

I stood in the dazzling sunlight of the plaza, watching the snow-covered peaks and the explosion of clouds rising up from the crest of the mountains. They seemed alive, an awesome presence brooding above the ancient village touched with light and energy. Along the ice-fringed creek that divided the two parts of the village, small Indian children played in the water; watching me suspiciously, yet never hesitating for a moment, Indian women glided down to the water with buckets, wearing brightly-colored shawls and high-topped white boots. Around the plaza, artists and photographers worked doggedly to capture the mystery of the village and the mountains and the women for they, along with myself, felt inadequate witnesses to a world at once private and universal. We needed to verify, to establish credentials against what we did not understand, yet tried to claim in some small way, as if it would make us wiser. For me, affirmation was in a small, black river stone that I carried for years, certain that it gave me knowledge.

Both the north and the south villages were oc-cupied then. A thin veil of blue smoke curled from a hundred chimneys, emitting the pungent fragrance of juniper that has been associated with New Mexico for centuries. On the rooftops old men stood wrapped in their blankets like mummies, watching the sky for hours at a time, their faces toward the sun. Every so often one of them would cry out the news of the day—this was before Taos Indians had telephones. Horse-drawn wagons carried loads of wood across the plaza, with whole families riding in the back on top of the logs, singing softly. Even then I realized that the Taos Indians lived on public display nearly every day of the year simply because of the fact that their pueblo, of all the nineteen along the Rio Grande, is the most beautiful and serene, an Indian Brigadoon that beckoned to restless individuals like myself who had rejected the excesses of their own culture. That Taos Pueblo was locked in a 50-year-long battle with the Forest Service over the return of their sacred Blue Lake was not obvious that day. The deceptive serenity of the Pueblo was then, as now, a way for the Indians to conceal the frustrations of their lives.

On this first visit, I met an old Indian man who was to change my life. Fearful, hesitant, wondering if he would think me hopeless, I climbed the ladder to his second-floor house and found Ben Marcus and his wife, Manuelita. With his high cheekbones, hawklike nose, and regal bearing, he looked like the quintessential Indian made famous by Edward Curtis. Within a short time, Ben began explaining how dancing ran in his blood. As he talked, his moccasined feet tapped out a steady rhythm on the worn linoleum floor. Later, I found out from

Emily and Eliseo Concha on their fiftieth wedding anniversary.

Manuelita that Ben loved dancing so much that sometimes he got up early in the morning and danced all by himself out on his rooftop.

Soon I met some of Ben and Manuelita's family—their introspective son Frank, his outgoing wife, Josephine, and their three small children, Frankie, Jerome, and Leticia. Ben and his wife also had a younger son named Joe David, who lived in Colorado Springs, as well as three daughters—Marie, Sally, and Juanita, who lived at the pueblo with their families. All of them were gifted dancers, especially four-year-old Frankie, who possessed an exquisite grace even then. Dancing was a way for this family to become connected with the earth, to draw renewal from thirty generations of ancestors who had lived in this same magnificent place.

As I left I stood on the rooftop of the Marcus house, watching the light play on the looming mountains to the north. A red-tailed hawk soared majestically toward the steep canyons and the trees. Although it was spring, snow still blanketed Taos Mountain, more than 12,000 feet high. Great shafts of amber light struck the thick adobe walls of the village, filtering the ever-present dust with luminosity. Below me, dozens of Indians hurried across the plaza, the men in blankets, the women in shawls; they seemed part of a vast, moving Technicolor dream that might vanish at any moment. The place was ethereal and it seemed to me as I stood there that a deep, old presence emanated from those ancient pueblo walls.

Something happened to me then. I began to feel a kinship with the Indian people, the land, and the sky of northern New Mexico. It was as if I'd been there before, so familiar did it seem. After that, I visited Taos Pueblo often, sometimes to chat with Ben Marcus, at other times to go up into the mountains with him and his family, to gather wood, to picnic, or to sit quietly by a stream, listening to the wind and the water. Always there were stories or a single powerful line that stuck in my mind. I remember, a few years before he died, when Ben Marcus, exhausted from a day hoeing corn, turned and said, "I am old now and covered with my life." The old man had been my friend and teacher for nearly twenty-five years.

The Marcus family visited me at my home in Colorado Springs when they came to town for pow-wows. Sometimes six or seven family members would arrive late at night, go upstairs, and lay out their bedrolls on the floor of my daughter Karin's room as she slept. (As she said years later, "I never knew if I was going to wake up and find a room full of Indians.") In the morning we all met for breakfast in my kitchen, Manuelita Marcus frying the homemade tortillas she had brought along. The Marcus children played happily with mine, though my middle daughter, Kate, later confessed that she used to hide under the bed because she was terrified that Jerome Marcus, then six, was going to scalp her.

During this period I also met Josephine Marcus's parents, Emily and Eliseo Concha. He was a tall, dignified shop teacher at the Day School; she was a hardworking nurse's aide at the clinic. They lived behind the main village, across the street from Frank and Josephine, in a rambling adobe house that Eliseo built for Emily in 1934, the year they were married. There was an apple orchard in the back and, attached to the house, two adobe ovens that Emily used for baking bread. Sometimes we all piled into Eliseo's pickup and went up to their ranch in the mountains, where Eliseo had a large garden, first planted by his grandfather long years before. A cold, clear stream ran beside the cabin, singing a throaty song. Here the old couple slept under a lean-to, in an old bed with a sagging mattress, so they could hear the stream sing. For fifty-two years they came to this place and watched their family grow. Eliseo left parts of himself here and there—a brush shelter in the forest, the skull of a deer hung on a fence post, his initials etched into the concrete steps going down to the stream; his paths crisscrossed the mountain that he loved, deep into the trees and out again. It was his place, and after he died, I felt his presence each time that I returned.

The view of the Rio Grande Valley was spectacular from Eliseo's ranch, and I used to imagine what it was like four hundred years ago when the first conquistadores rode up the valley. In the hush of golden afternoons we looked for eagles soaring above the peaks; we observed deer moving down the slopes to the meadow beside the cabin and heard the call of coyotes in the distance. Some-

Frank Marcus, Jr., chases his wife, Juana, during a water fight at Eliseo Concha's ranch.

times Eliseo fished for trout in his stream, drawing enormous pleasure from showing his grandsons how to bait a hook. One fall I helped him harvest his corn, squash, and pumpkins for what turned out to be the last time. The infirmities of old age kept him from planting his extensive garden again, but he watched as Frank and his grandsons planted, hoed, and irrigated, just like always. This closely knit family welcomed me into their midst year after year, and the bonds of friendship grew.

Gradually, I began to write about what I was feeling. I had never written a poem before but in 1971, after ten years of learning from the Taos Indians, I wrote a book of poetry called *Hollering Sun*. When it appeared, Joe David Marcus said, "Maybe no white man will ever understand these poems, but an Indian will." It was the ultimate compliment from a man who offers few compliments. But I wanted to go deeper.

I wrote another book of poetry, *Many Winters*, that examined such themes as old age, death, love, and regeneration. After that I retreated to the high mountains near timberline and wrote an allegorical tale, *The Man Who Gave Thunder to the Earth*, based on Ben Marcus's life. By then I felt deeply connected to Taos Pueblo and to the magic of northern New Mexico. My life in Colorado Springs was over, but I did not accept this for several more years.

Although I'd been a photographer since 1975, I didn't take any photographs of Taos Pueblo until 1984. I simply wasn't ready. One cold March day that year a strange thing happened. I woke up in the middle of the night in Colorado Springs, unable to sleep, my heart pounding. Something drew me to Taos Pueblo, 225 miles away, at four o'clock in the morning during a blizzard. I arrived at nine thirty to find a grieving Marcus family gathered around the kitchen table. "We just buried Ben," Frank Marcus said.

At that point I decided to make an in-depth study, in words and photographs, of everyday life at the Pueblo. So many changes had occurred since my first visit in 1961 that I wanted to capture what was left before it was too late. The idea gripped me like no other; for months I thought of little else. But it was impractical, if not impossible.

My life had changed when India, the last of my four children, went off to college in 1984. I was free at last, ready to explore a different sort of reality. Why not move to Taos? Confident yet apprehensive, I sold my house in Colorado Springs and simply moved south, using my real estate proceeds in order to stay alive. Soon I was photographing weddings, birthdays, anniversaries, baptisms, and feast days at the request of the families involved. In return I supplied them with inexpensive color prints, shot at the same time. However, I needed access to the Pueblo at times when tourists were not around. Quiet, dignified Santana Romero, then Pueblo governor, understood what I was trying to do. He gave me an open pass to the village, as well as an admonition: Don't photograph anyone unless they want you to.

As I photographed, I realized that no one had ever been permitted to make such a record of Taos Pueblo life before. Quite probably, no one would do so again. I had been given a priceless opportunity to document this changing culture, a privilege that both frightened and inspired me. I thought of Edward Curtis and what he had done there early in the century, as well as Laura Gilpin's

work shot over a thirty-year period. Ansel Adams had tried his hand at the Pueblo; so, too, had Paul Strand. But no one, as far as I knew, was allowed beyond the pueblo walls where most of the Indians lived.

Over a five-year period, I shot more than six thousand photographs of everyday Taos Pueblo life. I became interested in the differences between generations, how they dressed and wore their hair, the sorts of houses they lived in, the kinds of vehicles they drove, as well as what they did at home. Remembering my long association with Roy Stryker, director of the famed FSA (Farm Security Administration) photographic project of the 1930s, I looked for what he called "the significant detail"—backyards, outhouses, ovens, a gas pump, footwear—all those cultural details that add character to a subject. Even now, I'm not finished. It would take another twenty-seven years, at least.

During the past quarter century, I've become close to many people at the Pueblo and listened to their stories about the death of loved ones, the changing role of women, the loss of language, the corruption of tribal values, as well as what they cherish most about their lives. These are powerful and highly original statements, straight from the heart. Sometimes, as when a woman told me about the death of her young daughter in a motorcycle accident, I came home and wept. Then I thought about her stoicism. I realized, finally, *that* was what she wanted me to feel, not sorrow or pity.

For many years, the Taos have permitted me a rare look into very special parts of their lives. One cold, dreary November morning, as lightning cracked across the sky, I walked from the church to the cemetery with the Indian people to honor their dead on All Souls' Day. This is the only day of the year when the Taos are allowed in the cemetery, except for burials. The church bells had tolled mournfully all night long; now, as the rain fell in a steady drizzle, the people walked along the alleyway in their finest clothing, carrying flowers, fruit, and candles. Up and down the rows of handmade crosses they went and when they found their relatives, they knelt in the mud and lovingly placed their offerings and lit their candles. A soft crying swept across the rows of graves, some new, some old, some merely a pile of stones. Those who had died during the previous year were remembered with new crosses. Back and forth the Indians went in the cemetery, in a profoundly moving ceremony of love and courage that touched me deeply. Then, as is the custom, people drifted away to their village houses, there to eat a traditional meal of chili, stew, bread, coffee, and bread pudding. During this interlude, the pueblo was closed to all non-Indians, except those like myself who had been specially invited.

There have been other memorable times, too. The night that my "Indian granddaughter" Maria Ann Thompson was born in 1983, my old friends, Frank and Josephine Marcus, and I waited at the hospital until we knew that mother and daughter were fine, then I took the new grandparents out for a champagne celebration. The day that I was initiated into the Marcus family by being thrown into the creek at Eliseo's ranch. The time that I was invited to an Indian-only celebration following their kiva "graduation," an ancient, sacred ritual wherein lies the heart of Pueblo religion.

We have had our sadness as well, such as the time that Josephine found out she had breast cancer. She, Leticia, and I sat in the doctor's office, and heard the verdict, Josephine the only one without a trace of fear. She went through radiation therapy, brave and uncomplaining, then resumed her busy life as if nothing in the world had happened.

There are many moments with the Indians that are especially dear to me. I remember the day that Red Shirt Reyna took me fishing on my birthday and told me hilarious childhood stories as he cooked six trout over a piñon fire—and later produced two cookies in lieu of a birthday cake. I remember how eighty-five-year-old John Concha, Eliseo's older brother, carefully put on his best Pendleton blanket and played me some old Indian songs on his favorite drum and I remember half a dozen wistful marriage proposals from lonely old Indian men.

One day I took Marie Mondragon to the mountains to look for Indian tea and she began to sing an old corn-grinding song as she wandered through the forest, her arms filled with wild flowers. One September, Josephine fell down a ladder and broke her leg and asked me to help her prepare the feast for San Geronimo Day—chili, posole, sopa—in quantities large enough to feed a regiment. Then there was the day she tried to show me how to plaster an adobe wall. The gooey mess just kept falling off on the ground. Nor have I been successful at learning to bake Indian bread, though numerous Pueblo women have tried to show me how to mix a hundred pounds of flour, a couple of handsful of salt, about this much lard, a ladleful or two of water, optional eggs, and a few packets of yeast. Shape into five hundred loaves and bake for a certain time (just look at the sun) in an oven without a thermometer (test with a piece of straw).

Like other Pueblo tribes, the Taos are gracious, hospitable people. They never turn anyone away from their table, even a stranger who might wander

Maria Ann Thompson.

in the door by accident. For years I've been part of numerous family celebrations—birthdays, anniversaries, weddings—and even funerals, where there is always food after the burial. After Eliseo's funeral, we gathered at the family's pueblo house, there to share our sorrow, as well as our remembrance of a rich, full life. I remembered the old man sitting at the edge of his field, listening to his corn grow. On the night of January 6, when the pueblo is closed to outsiders, the Indians go from house to house and dance, sometimes in outlandish costumes meant for fun. This is a time of warmth and camaraderie that I have been privileged to witness several times, accompanied by my Indian friends.

How magnificent is Christmas Eve—the huge bonfires, the procession around the plaza, and the alabados—hymns—rising up and up to the flaming sky. I'm always invited to the Marcus family dinner that follows afterward, then to another dinner on Christmas Day, when there is either a Deer Dance or Los Matachines (introduced by the Spanish), and friend after friend invites me in to eat. The same is true of San Geronimo Day, where I once ate nine dinners between nine a.m. and noon. These are the precious moments of shared joy that I will remember all my life.

Nor will I forget all the other wonderful gifts the Indians have given me: dozens of loaves of bread, bundles of Indian tea, a broom made of rabbit brush, roasted chilis, beaded jewelry, strings of ceremonial corn, traditional Taos pottery, and a lovely heart-shaped drum, inscribed: "Nancy—Remember, I'm only a heartbeat away." Above all, I remember the daily gifts they gave me. Unconditional love. Acceptance. An obdurate, persistent patience. Consistency. Generosity of spirit.

The Taos Indians are a permanent part of my life. They've helped me achieve a quiet heart. I give them this book in appreciation for showing me the way to spiritual renewal that I searched for so many years ago.

Nancy Wood
Taos, New Mexico
August 1988

Acknowledgments

No book of this kind can be successfully completed without the love and support of many people. I would like to thank those who worked hard in the processing and printing of my photographs: Eddie and Elfreide Dyba of San Francisco; Kelley Kirkpatrick and Rod Hook of Santa Fe; Gordon Adams of Taos; and Alan Hazlett of Colorado Springs. They made thousands of prints and contact sheets for me over a five-year period.

For their critical reading of the manuscript I would like to thank Carolyn Johnston, Karen Embertson, Vine Deloria, Jr., Tony Frank Martinez, R.C. Gordon-McCutcheon, John and Mary Collier, Mary Jacqueline Trussell, and Karen Schwehn. My friend Robert Parker kept me going during the entire project, enriched my outlook, and was of vital importance in the preliminary editing of both text and photographs. Nancy Johnson pitched in on the home front whenever I needed her.

A photography grant from the Maytag Foundation helped launch the project in 1984. A literary fellowship from the National Endowment for the Arts in 1987 enabled me to complete the research and writing without pressure. The Museum of Indian Arts and Culture in Santa Fe exhibited fifty-five of my prints during its inaugural exhibition in 1987. Thanks especially to Rachelle Hansen and Arthur Nolan of the Pentax Corporation, which generously donated my camera equipment—the Pentax 645 and two LS II's, complete with lenses and accessories. Tal Luther of Taos provided access to his vast library of southwestern history.

My editor, Lee Goerner, a man who loves the Southwest, has been a source of encouragement and helpful criticism throughout. My agent, Gail Hochman of Brandt and Brandt, believed in the book even in its early stages. I wish also to express my deepest gratitude to the Taos Indians for sharing their hopes, fears, and dreams.

TAOS PUEBLO

Overleaf: *Ruined mission church and cemetery with homemade wooden crosses.*

Chapter One ORIGINS

It's hard being an Indian. You have to live three lives—the traditional one, the survival one, and the modern world that keeps coming at you all the time.
ROSE ALBERT, *Taos Pueblo*, 1986

The only thing that holds us together is our religion, but I wonder if it will last. It's not just a religion, like the Catholic religion. God doesn't mean fear. He means the Creator, the One Above. The mountains over there. The sky above. It's Mother Earth. The stories we learned as children were about God meaning love and God meaning beauty, just as it is in nature everywhere around you. There is no church because all is a church to us here.
TONY FRANK MARTINEZ, *Taos Pueblo*, 1986

Francisco Martinez, 107 years old, also known as Cradle of the Deer. He was an important religious leader.

Time and memory encapsulate the people of Taos Pueblo and hold them to ancestral lands like parentheses. They are frozen in a million yesterdays. The sunbaked New Mexico landscape has infused the people with grit and given them a far-reaching tenacity, like trees or rocks. To the north, sacred Taos Mountain (Mon'whalo) looms above the old village, witness to seven centuries of drumbeats and moccasined feet wearing a neutral sweetness into the earth. The mountain and the village are embedded in the blood as well as in the memory of fifteen hundred Indians who claim Taos Pueblo as their own.

Other sacred mountains are part of this sweeping southern Sangre de Cristo chain—Flute (Tuptú), Bluebird Tail (Sulwétuna), and Bow (Wilpiánta), each having its own religious significance and history within the network of tribal lore. Here great hunts for deer and elk once took place; here the eagle was reverently captured for his feathers; here the huge Stone Men fell and became part of Pueblo mythology. Here above all is Blue Lake (P'achale), the sacred and serene turquoise jewel high on the uppermost flank of Taos Mountain, from which the Indians believe they came in a time before time that only they can explain. Here, too, are ancient paths worn through dense forests of aspen and fir, holy shrines beside a waterfall or in a meadow where a rock heap resembles a family of bears. Spirits dwell in every tree and flower, in every rock and stream, in animals and birds as well. Time and again the Indian is healed in these places; he can endure the worst of times because of these unconditional gifts.

West of the Pueblo lies the stark and mystical Rio Grande Valley, a vast table of lava spewed forth by ancient volcanoes, then cut in two by a mighty river rising from the north. The Spanish named it El Rio Bravo. The Indians didn't name it anything. In the old days the river with its deep, winding gorge was a natural boundary. Beyond it lay the domain of the feared and hated Apaches and Navajos. More vicious than either of these were the merciless Utes, who swept in from the northwest to steal from the Taos their wives and children to trade to the Spanish for horses (three strong women were said to be worth one stallion in those days). One day a decisive battle took place on the windswept grassland above the river. The Taos ambushed their Ute enemies and hurled them over the cliff, 500 feet down to the river. Even today, a lingering animosity exists between the wary Taos and their Ute brothers, based on grievances at least two hundred and fifty years old.

The light in northern New Mexico is pure and crystalline, as if the sun simply exploded from its own intensity. The sun locks the land in dryness, cracks it open and exposes the vulnerability of nature in a relentless process of epochal change. Even in winter, the sun is fierce, searing the landscape as well as the mind; memory is locked in a time when there was only an unspoiled land so vast a man could not reach the end of it in his lifetime. At night, the spirits of bears and wolves and eagles and coyotes move about, offering encouragement. Here the star-filled sky presses down on the blackness of the land, as if to impose its greater power on the fragility of the earth. The land of the Taos Indians sweeps the mind clean of societal clutter and forces an inevitable confrontation between the dualities of the inner and outer life. One must eventually choose.

A long time ago, the Taos chose this place—or the place chose them. According to one commonly accepted tribal legend, the Sun and Moon once mated above Blue Lake. While all the stars of the heavens watched, the People spilled out between the Sun and Moon, sliding down the handle of the Big Dipper into the water. There they lived for a while in the Underworld, acquiring wisdom and knowledge. Then they came up through the lake's watery navel and stood on dry ground, looking around. The Feather People (Fiadaina) emerged first and went south, to a home near Ranchos de Taos, where they built a village of mud. Then the Shell People (Holdaina) emerged and made their way to Red River, twenty miles north, thence to Pot Creek, about fifteen miles south. The Water People (Badaine) came next and became fish who swam in the Ranchos de Taos Creek until observed by a girl of the Feather Clan. She ran to tell her people, and when they returned, the fish were standing up in the water. Two girls struck the fish with two bean plants and they became people.

These three clans introduced themselves and together they went back to Taos Mountain to await the arrival of the other clans as they emerged from Blue Lake, one at a time. The Big Earring People (Fialusladaina), the Old Ax People (Fiadaikwaslauna), and the Knife People (Chiadaina) came out of the water and admired the beauty of the sky and trees, the waterfalls and the grass, the moon and stars. As the clans grew used to their new surroundings, the four-legged animals became brothers; streams became veins of life; the stars offered company at night; hawks and eagles presented them with the idea of majesty. But soon the clans grew hungry, for they had been eating nothing but nuts and berries; they did not know how to hunt. One day, a sacred deer came out of the forest. He showed them how to make a bow and arrows. When they were finished,

Entrance to Taos Pueblo.

Adobe wall and oven.

the deer stood there and said, "Now you must shoot me in order to have meat." After that, the Taos never went hungry again.

According to one legend, parts of each clan eventually became other tribes: the Feather People gave birth to the Navajos, the Old Ax People became the Plains Indians, the Water People produced the Eskimos. Mohawks, Apaches, Utes, Hopis, Comanches, and Pueblo tribes all evolved from that primordial time when the Taos were exploring the new and magical world of nature, delighting in ants and butterflies, leaves and rushing water, crimson sunsets and the purity of each golden dawn. This wisdom traveled with the newborn tribes when they departed north, south, east, and west, leaving the Taos alone on the mountain of their origin. Even then, they knew they were the center of the universe and that when the world was destroyed, they alone would survive because of their superior skills and knowledge.

One day when the weather became cold, the ancient people called Yuanahentsai came down the mountain to the Place of the Red Willow (Yahlahaaimu-bahutulba). The river from Blue Lake flowed through a lush meadow filled with waist-high grass, so the people took it as a sign. Half of them took their skins and points and stone tools and went to the north side of the river, half to the south side. They built two villages out of Mother Earth, mixing the dirt with water from the sacred river to make it strong. The villages grew higher and higher, one story upon another, until at last they looked like mountains. The village on the north side they

Tribally owned buffalo herd roams the grassland west of the village.

called Hlauuoma (Cold Elevated); the village on the south side Hlauk-wima (Cold Diminished). Each clan became part of a kiva, an underground ceremonial chamber, on either side of the river, and they began to gather the stories, beliefs, and rituals that would sustain the culture. Wise men began to notice the exact travels of Sun, Moon, and stars and made their marks on blackened kiva walls. From their observations, they divided the year into twelve parts and called them:

December, Night Fire Moon: Nuúpapana

January, Man Moon: Söenpana

February, Wind Big Moon: Walapana

March, Ash Moon: Naxöpana

April, Planting Moon: Kapana

May, Corn Planting Moon: Iakápana

June, Corn Tassel Coming Out Moon: Kapnákoyapana

July, Sun House Moon: Tultöpana

August, Lake Moon: Paw'epana

September, Corn Ripe Moon: Iaköwapana

October, Leaves Falling Moon: Ölulpana

November, Corn Depositing Moon: Iatayæpana

Overleaf: Pueblo Peak, also called Taos Mountain, 12,305 feet high.

When he saw that the Taos people were of good spirit, the Sun Father blessed them and the Four Wind Brothers blew in rain to water crops of corn, beans, and squash carefully planted in the fields beyond the village according to the exact positions of the sun and moon. Dances arose from a need for mystery and supplication, songs grew from the expanding hearts of those in love with their surroundings. Stories exploded out of experience and were passed on to illustrate the need for courage, unity, practicality, patience, and humility. The people moved evenly together; their knowledge grew far beyond the confines of their village, as far south as Mexico. Eventually everyone was divided into fourteen clans, which exist to the present day. Among them are Big Hail People, Day People or Sun People, Knife People, Water Dripping People, Water People or Lightning, Old Axe or Corn Meal, elemental names that connect them to the gray antiquity of their origins.

The Taos are divided as well into moieties or halves. Those who live on the north side are the Winter People (Tuin t'aine) ; those on the south side, the Summer People (Tulte t'aine). The rivalry between the two sides is best evidenced through the foot races, held each May 3, the beginning of the planting season, and again on September 30, when harvest traditionally ends. The races are dramatic enactments of a ritual as old as the Pueblo itself. There in the chilly predawn, with the mountain drenched in shadows and the village peaceful in the pewter-colored light, two lines of nearly naked men come out of their kivas on either side of the river and, singing softly, move to opposite ends of the race track. Their dark hair is loose and flowing, their bodies and faces are painted with white and red stripes, and on their torsos are glued the down of the hawk to ensure swiftness. A tribal integrity going back before Christ, before Moses, even perhaps before the pyramids is inherent in these runners who the next day will return to being postal clerks, truck drivers, backhoe operators, clerks, students, artisans, shopkeepers, or the unemployed. But for this day they are like winged gods. This ritual, like all others at Taos Pueblo, may not be photographed, though photographs were permitted in an earlier time.

As the sun breaks over the mountains, as many as two hundred males between the ages of six and sixty race back and forth against each other to encourage the Father Sun on his eternal course through the sky. The runners, wearing only breechcloths, intimate to the Cloud People, the Surpassing People of the Middle Heaven, how they should also seasonally race across the sky to bring the growing rains. Most runners race barefoot over the rough, hard ground to demonstrate their resistance to pain; to fall indicates that the runner is not right in his heart. A period of prayer and introspection follows.

The foot race is not based on speed and endurance as much as it is on the religious fervor of the participants, who claim that they lose all consciousness of the world about them as they become the human link

Clowns, called chiffonetti *or* chipuna, *climb the pole to reach a bounty of food and a freshly slaughtered sheep,* 1902. (H. S. Poley, Denver Public Library, Western History Department)

between earth and sky, sun and moon, and the ever-moving cycle of the seasons. As James Lujan, a Taos living in Albuquerque, put it, "The foot races are literally a race for life. We believe that long ago the world ended when the Sun God fell to the earth at the north end of the race track, plunging the world into total darkness. The foot races are run to draw power and strength from the sun to enable us to survive as a tribe."

Century after century, origins were manifest in daily life, hands joined together in war and labor and love, reaffirmation in the same plowed fields, the return of the meadow larks, the grinding of corn, the men who watched the sun, making notches in stone about its ineluctable progress north to south, south to north, on the same path always. But it required the individual faith of men to make it happen, the collective belief of the whole tribe to coax the sun back home again. So was natural law verified. When the Spanish arrived in the sixteenth century, submission to crown and cross came not from any sincere conversion to Catholicism, but rather through a brutal system of tribute that turned the people into slaves for their Spanish masters. Through it all, they remained rooted to the land and beliefs of their origins. Every aspect of daily life, no matter how simple, had some sort of religious significance, and does to the present

Foot races, San Geronimo Day, circa 1910. (Smithsonian Institution)

Traffic jam on San Geronimo Day, 1897.
(Denver Public Library, Western History
Department)

day. To the Taos, even an insect is sacred; so, too, is every bird, and all the animals. Corn is highly sacred, as is pollen, for they bring life. The four directions have deep religious meaning, as do the four winds, the clouds, the stars, the moon, and most powerful of all, the sun and earth.

Sharon Reyna, a thirty-five-year-old potter, says, "Making a pot has religious significance for me. When I go to get my clay, I always leave a little something for the earth when I go there. A cracker. Cheese. Even beer. The earth is good to me—it lets me take the clay. There is a ritual to it—giving something back as you take something away. If I didn't do this, I don't think my pots would be any good.

"For other people making drums, making moccasins, doing beadwork, making bread, or plastering are all connected to something from the earth. Moccasin makers and drum makers use deer hide. The deer has to die in order to make the moccasins, the drum. So it's part asking the animal to sacrifice himself to this work, part asking that his spirit enter the piece. In pottery, you try and capture the spirit of the earth, the mystery, the goodness. You ask the spirit of the earth to stay in the pot, to bring good fortune and long life to whoever uses it."

Perhaps it is the sprawling adobe architecture of this seven-hundred-year-old village, four and five stories high, that suggests unbroken tradi-

tion, long tenure on the land, blood that still courses with memories of primordial secrets. Perhaps it is only a fiction that has arisen here, out of smoke and ashes, mirrored by those tribespeople who believe the enduring mythology about themselves. What is real and not real is divided by a thin line between memory and history uttered in the endangered Tiwa tongue, native to the Taos as well as to their Picuris cousins on the other side of the mountains.

The shadow of spiritual expression lurks in the immutable faces of old men wrapped in cotton blankets as thin and durable as their own skin. They stride across the hard crusted earth of the plaza, anxious to preserve the meaning of old times. In their troubled eyes are reflected the contours of mountains, eagle wings, standing bears, and buffalo. Their

A cross made of aspen leaves sits atop a bower where santos from the church are carried to watch the foot races along with the priest, the Pueblo governor, and other dignitaries on San Geronimo Day.

stories and the stories of their grandfathers before them are repeated in the six sacred kivas where the heart of Taos Pueblo religion beats on, year after year, century after century. Small boys listen to these stories, not always understanding the meaning, only that it is up to them to become guardians of communal integrity. Against a frightening backdrop of cosmic catastrophe, irreversible pollution, and death-dealing technology, a fragile, archaic system of belief manages to comfort and sustain an anachronistic group of people immersed in rapid cultural change.

Santana "Sam" Romero is a respected Taos Pueblo elder, a recent governor who waited all his life for the honor, bestowed not through general election but by a council of elders, a process that has been in existence more than two hundred years. One morning he sat in the living room of a well-kept trailer home he shares with his wife, Senaida, a nurse at the Taos hospital. He described what made him tough enough to become a leader of his people.

"I survived the Bataan Death March," he says proudly, his two long braids wrapped in blue felt. His round face is unlined and faintly cherubic; he does not look seventy-three years old. "Then I had four years in a Japanese prisoner-of-war camp. I went to hell and then came back. It's not for humans what I went through. I worked in a copper mine with two hundred and fifty men. About half survived. I got down to one hundred pounds. To keep myself alive I sang songs [in the Tiwa language]. I told myself stories I learned as a boy. I dreamed about my home, my people. I said, God, give me a chance to be a leader or a chief. I don't care how stupid I am, just let me survive."

Like many returning Pueblo veterans, Sam Romero was forced to find work out of town because few jobs were available in Taos. Like many Indians, he believes that Hispanics are given preference in a predominantly Hispanic town where tempers often flare between the two cultures over something as insignificant as a parking space. Romero was a construction worker in Colorado for more than twenty years, though he returned home regularly to participate in his kiva "doings." In 1986, he was finally elected governor, a position that he used to try and help his tribe become economically self-sufficient by unveiling an ambitious plan for a golf course and convention center overlooking the Rio Grande gorge.

While implementation of such a plan may prove unfeasible, Romero was the first governor to think on a grand scale. His ideas for better public relations resulted in a popular summer guide service where pueblo women escort visitors around the village, telling of their history. Today Sam Romero is an important man in his kiva where his main job is the education of young boys in the same tribal ways taught to *him* years ago by his elders. He sees life as a series of concentric circles, each one building upon another to form the strong yet fragile link that has held his people

Former Pueblo Governor Santana Romero
and his wife, Senaida.

Leticia Thompson and her father, Frank
Marcus, Pueblo fire chief.

together since the beginning. But now, he notices certain changes. Settling into his favorite chair, he shakes his head sadly and clasps his hands.

"In the old days, long ago, we used to have all that land in the mountains, all of it sacred," he says. "We had our gods up there, our shrines. Every August we'd go up, the same as we do now. To this lake, to that lake, for a different reason. We got Blue Lake back, but the rest are gone, except we still see them in our minds."

His face is smooth, but the years have worn a certain tenacity into it. "Everything is changing, just in my lifetime," he continues. "People moving out of the village, so they're not together anymore. All these new [Housing and Urban Development, or HUD] houses going up, just like Albuquerque, Denver. No more farming, so we don't grow our own food. We're sick from the white man's food. Our language is being forgotten, too. You can't find many young people who speak it, only old people like me. We're even starting to speak English in the kivas now, so some of the boys will understand. I was against it. I said, Let them learn the language, but some of the older ones said, It's the only way they'll learn. It hurt me to see it happen, but what could I do? I'm the head man now [in his kiva], for the rest of my life. It's up to me to tell these little boys the way it is. Some of them don't believe it anymore, very few really do. So I get after them. I say, You're just like a white man now. You're stupid.

"I have a few boys though, nine or ten years old, who speak good Indian. They want to learn the old ways. They listen to the old stories. I'll tell them what my grandfathers taught me. I didn't have a son, only one girl. So these boys are like my own. Someday when I'm gone, one of them will take over. That's how we pass it on. I don't think our religion will ever die out." He estimates that 90% of all Pueblo boys between five and twelve years old are in kiva training.

However, the usage of English in the kivas has dangerous implications for the tribe. If all six kivas eventually adopted English, not only would the untranslatable meaning behind old stories be lost, but also the precious secrecy that protects Taos Pueblo religion from the outside world. "Our language is our last defense," an Indian friend once told me, meaning that Tiwa is the only way to preserve tribal integrity and autonomy. Indeed, a language even older than Tiwa is spoken in the kivas by elders who converse only among themselves. So precious is language to the Taos that when a class in Tiwa was offered at the Day School and a handful of curious Anglos showed up, the Indians canceled the course.

Outsiders will never fully understand what makes the Taos Indians tick, nor do the natives share their sacred knowledge with anyone except themselves. Like every other tribe in America which has seen its land, water, and freedom stolen by European invaders, the Taos have only one resource left—their spiritual traditions. To protect this legacy, they will relate all manner of tales about themselves, which may or may not be true.

The Taos Pueblo powwow is an annual event, where tribes from all over North America gather to compete for thousands of dollars' worth of prize money and to renew old ties.

Evan Trujillo, a prize-winning dancer, has been dancing since he was two.

Billy Jo Concha, right, waits her turn with two Plains Indian women.

Sonny Spruce pauses during a break in dancing at the Pueblo Day School.

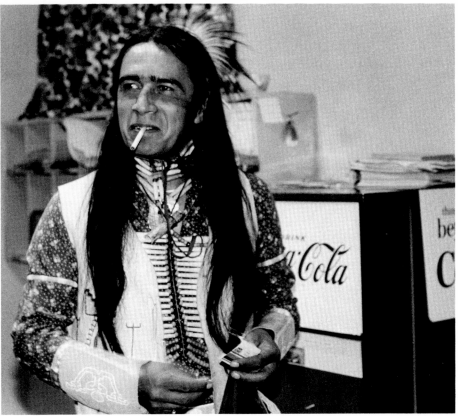

Above, left to right: Richard Brown,
Sonny Spruce, and Stephen Mondragon.

A young contestant competes in the girls'
fancy shawl dance.

One tribal elder, who did not want his name used, told me, "In the very first round, Noah came in the ark. No Indians were here then, just earth, trees, water. Noah brought the animals—the bear, the deer, the elk, the birds, everything we used later on. He landed on Sandia Peak [near Albuquerque], and the animals came out of the ark and spread all over the land. After that, the people came out of Blue Lake. They found the animals that Noah had brought, waiting for them right here. In the round after that, the Taos people could run like deer or hunt like coyotes. They could fly like birds. They could communicate with one another, just like a telephone."

Another respected leader says, "We had television back then. We

23   *Origins*

could see what was going on in Michigan, and they could see us. There were gods here then who could fly from place to place like a rocket. When man went to the moon, he became like a god, and the real gods didn't like it. That's why you have so much trouble now."

Another Taos Pueblo man says he does not believe his people came out of Blue Lake or that Noah landed nearby either. He says the truth is that the Taos came from outer space, speaking a version of Latin now uttered only in the kivas during certain religious ceremonials.

While the Taos remain secretive about their origin stories, non-Indians want chronological facts about origins and experiences. Archaeologists have spent their careers trying to figure out how the Taos got to this particular spot in New Mexico before it was part of Mexico or before that, part of Spain, or had any particular name at all. In those days, nomadic tribes roamed the vast Rio Grande Valley as Pit House Dwellers, some settling in the natural caves of the Colorado Plateau. Pyramid house heaps were constructed on mesa tops, close to the sun. There the people wove blankets out of turkey feathers, made sandals from yucca stalks, ate the milpa of corn, beans, and squash, traded with other tribes from as far south as central Mexico, fought one another, and eventually disappeared. Silent ruins attest to vanished civilizations; pottery shards splashed with black or red paint signify a living presence; stories etched in rock describe a vivid history, mythical or not; old bones, recently discovered, indicate an inexplicable cannibalism among a people presumably peaceful. Who were the Taos?

One version of Indian prehistory contends that the Taos came from the Colorado and New Mexico cliff dwellings to the north and west, wandered southwest by way of the Chama River, and joined other Indians at Abiquiu. They built a pueblo at Ojo Caliente and long years passed. Then an unknown something moved them south again, to Black Mountain in what is now western Arizona. Decade melted into decade, century into century. A Taos doesn't count time except by seasons and moons, harvests and hunts. What is a man's lifetime, he will say, except so many steps upon the earth? Or as a link between generations? Or for the purpose of carrying the thread of life across mountains and deserts and mesas, down through so many harvests that he cannot count them all?

Time passed at Black Mountain until perhaps there was a sickness or a drought or a famine. Perhaps a warring tribe drove them out. The Indian doesn't much care about details of departure either. This time they went north, marching slowly, for by then they had large numbers of domesticated turkeys which they drove before them. Stopping on the way, they built a new pueblo and lived for several generations or more. Long enough to keep the thread running. Long enough to leave their footprints on the earth.

Traveling north again, these ancestral Indians came to a place of abundant food and water. Here part of the tribe decided to stay, and they

Men's fancy dance contest attracts competitors from other pueblos in New Mexico.

became the Picuris (Wilana), still linguistically connected to the Taos. The other part of the tribe moved northwest into the Rio Grande Valley and settled on the Llano Quemado mesa fifteen miles south of the present pueblo. (This theory is consistent with the emergence myth as well as with scientific data.) Here the Indians were known as the People of the Swift-Coming Rain; their village was called Fiataid-hepuanay (Where the Feather People Lived). Many archaeologists believe that these were the forebears of the present-day Taos, who moved to their present site around A.D. 1250.

Still other anthropologists are convinced that the Taos descended from the Maya who fled north from the Yucatán during a period of warfare; others claim they evolved in part from the aborigines who moved south after a late crossing of the Bering Strait and became part of the Athapascan strain, evident in the physical features of the Taos today. The Mormons believe the Indians are the lost tribe of Israel who traveled across the ocean in a Phoenician-style ship after Moses cast them out of the Promised Land; one group, including the Taos, wandered out from the east coast and set up housekeeping along the Rio Grande. Another theory claims that the Taos spun off from the Chinese when a far-traveling junk washed up on the Pacific shore. (The Taos, however, prefer to think that the Chinese are *their* descendants.)

Where does the legend end? Where do facts begin? The tantalizing ruins of ancient house walls are still visible at Llano Quemado, awaiting excavation. Here the circle of an early kiva has yet another wall within it, suggesting that the Indians returned to rebuild the home that their ancestors, for some unknown reason, had abandoned. Other pueblo walls, leveled but not quite lost, suggest a journey which mysteriously circled the valley around to the west by Las Cordovas, then flung north. An anthropological question mark. An archaeological puzzle. An Indian nonfact of life.

Scientists have seldom been permitted to make studies of Taos Pueblo simply because the Indians are not interested in public scrutiny of their very private world. They do not care about excavation, examination, or probing into fragments of their past. However, in 1961, the tribal council, after being convinced that their land-claims suit would be bolstered by "archaeological data," allowed one Dr. J. J. Brody to examine an ancient refuse mound and to excavate an ancestral ruin—for one day only. Working feverishly, he unearthed a few pots and some primitive tools, then he was barred from further discovery.

From their limited research scientists claim that the present village is no more than five hundred years old, the first village having been destroyed by hostile tribes around 1450, a century before Coronado's men converged on the tribe in 1540. Indeed, the buried remains of an old village lie less than a hundred yards northwest of the present one. Tops of old adobe walls poke out of the earth and large depressions, possibly ancient kivas, are visible among the weeds. One Taos Pueblo family lives virtually on top of these ruins.

Bertha Vigil, a large woman with close-cropped curly hair, has lived in the same adobe house all her life. It lies just outside the village walls in an area considered highly sacred. Bertha has just quit her job at Taco Bell where she was working for $3.35 an hour, seventy-five hours a week, no overtime. Her husband, John, a Tesuque Pueblo Indian, is unemployed. Her beautiful seventeen-year-old daughter, Yvonne, an award-winning runner and an honor student, serves as a cadet for the tribal police force. She has already put in more than two thousand hours of work as an unpaid volunteer and looks forward to attending a law enforcement academy. She says her life's work is in police service, preferably at Taos Pueblo, where she is regarded as one of the most outstanding high school seniors. Yvonne shows me her running trophies and her scrapbook; Bertha pulls out family pictures that include some of her mother, Marie, who lives with them. This is a modern, yet traditional family, tied deeply to old roots, old ways. Yvonne, who is also a Taos Pueblo princess this year, splits her cultural roots between her father's Tesuque tribe and her mother's Taos. "I'm the best of both," she laughs as she goes out in her trim-fitting police uniform, ready for a shift that will last most of the night.

Bertha Vigil sips her coffee as we sit and talk in the large, sunny living room of the house built by her father over half a century ago. Her daughter is her whole life, she tells me; they have never been apart for one night since the day she was born. "Every day I tell her something about her people. Who they were. Where they came from. How this whole area was once a village," she says, "even where our house is now. When my dad was building our house, he found a tiny skeleton, a little child wrapped up in a blanket. So we buried it ourselves in the cemetery." Bertha says that the old village was where the people lived for a long time until the Spanish came in 1610. "There was no wall or anything, only a village, one and two stories high," she says. Forced to build a church, the people revolted for the first time in 1640, killing the priest and burning the church. The offending group fled east. One version has the renegades joining the Mohawks in New York State; another version claims that they became part of the Kiowas, who later returned, bringing the Sun Dance with them. Indeed, the Plains influence is obvious in the facial features of many Taos Pueblo families who have intermarried with Plains Indians for centuries, adapting their dress, dance, and songs to their own.

The history of Taos Pueblo has as many different versions as there are people to repeat the stories. Bertha continues. "The people were afraid the Spanish would come back, so they built a new village and put a wall around it for protection," she says. "And sure enough the Spanish did come back and they made the people build another church, bigger than the one before. Some people resisted at first, just like in the old days, but there were so many of them and so few of us that after a while the church

Seventeen-year-old Yvonne Vigil is a Taos tribal policewoman, right, but she also participates in dances of her father's Tesuque tribe, left.

got built. The old village just fell to the ground, but it's still a sacred place to us. Our ancestors are buried in this ground. There are shrines here and there. We go there to pray. The race track runs down to the end of the field where the old kivas were. So when they talked about running electricity through here, a lot of people got upset. They fought it. They didn't want the place of our ancestors disturbed. But the young kids come in here at night and try to dig things up. Pottery. Arrowheads. Things they can sell. We catch them and send them home. But some of our older people are doing it, too."

Bertha Vigil claims that in addition to the ruined village, there is an even older site, about a mile east of the present village where the water tower and the Day School now stand. "The river has been in this place only for a little while," she says. "In the old days it was up there by the Day School, running between those two little hills. The village was there at the time, and so were the fields. There was a long drought—years and years—and finally the river dried up. There was no water anywhere around. The people were starving. Their crops all dried up. They prayed and waited, prayed and waited, hoping the river would come back.

"Pretty soon a river started to form up there at Blue Lake. It came down a different way, through the canyon, and it flowed this way, the place it is now. So the people moved the village down here. The new river is bigger than the one before. It never dries up, even in a drought. We bathe in this river and drink it and cook our food. Babies are put in this river when they're only a few days old. At certain times of the year, everyone bathes in it. We make our adobes from the river water, so they are strong. Our river is sacred to us. When the river goes, we will go too. That's what we believe." (A few months later, Bertha Vigil died of a heart attack. She was forty-four years old. Yvonne Vigil abandoned her plans for a career in police work and married a Hispanic youth from Taos.)

There is not a Taos Indian who is not completely grounded in the mysterious yet exquisitely simple religion of his ancestors. It is part of his consciousness, a palpable presence that never leaves, even at death. All actions proceed from this religion, for it happens to be the glue that holds the tribe together. Taos Pueblo religion is mainly a blueprint for life, manifest in a strict code of behavior and a range of daily activities based on mutual help and support. A common belief in the tribe, the use of the Tiwa language, and a shared history is inherent within this religious framework. Life lessons are learned through reverence and keen observation of a complex natural world every waking moment of the day. The old have a solemn obligation to pass on knowledge to the young, often in indirect ways. College counselor Howard Rainer recalls: "My grandfather was a high religious leader, but he did not announce himself. He would come into a room and everyone would fall silent. He taught them their ways in the kiva and by living as an example to them. He was a natural teacher. I remember when I was just a boy, I took him his lunch when he was working in the fields. He was standing there with a hoe, looking at his corn. He'd been working all morning and his hands were very rough. When I handed him his lunch, he took hold of mine and rubbed them. They were very soft. But my grandfather didn't say a word, he just handed me his hoe and walked away. I did the best I could, and I learned something that day. That's how all of us learned when we were growing up, from what our grandfathers taught us." Then he adds, "The final test of a leader is that he leaves behind him in other men the conviction and the will to carry on."

Small boys are still taught by their fathers, grandfathers, and uncles to preserve the ancient, indestructible thread that exists among these generations. Because of the great importance of old men as teachers, mentors, and living examples of the Pueblo way, the death of an elder is a time of sorrow for the whole village. In every household the elderly are venerated and few people are consigned to nursing homes, but are cared for by their families until they die, much as in certain Asiatic cultures. Ann

Pueblo horses graze on an ancient ash pile. South village is in background.

Martinez cared for her elderly father, Francisco, for ten years before he died at 108. Unable to speak because of a stroke, he lived in a partitioned-off part of the living room, surrounded by family members. Says Ann Martinez, "The reason my dad lived a long time is because we loved him. He couldn't talk, but we knew the way he felt about us." Such devotion is found throughout the Pueblo.

Taos religion is passed on through instruction, observation, and osmosis. The main difference between it and Catholicism is that Catholicism is based upon dogma and authority while Taos belief is grounded in the mysteries of the natural world. Taos religion rejects the idea of sin, heaven, and hell, has no written laws, offers no reward, requires no church, and does not condemn nonbelievers. It is, of course, more complex than that, involving the deep, sacred teachings of the kiva and a calendar of rituals and cosmic renewal rites keyed to the position of the sun. But there is another, relatively new expression of belief that has tried to attach itself to Taos religion—the Native American Church.

Jerome Sandoval is a heavyset man in his mid-forties, college educated, and a counselor with the state Department of Education. As he says, "I live in three different worlds. When I'm here on the reservation, I'm an Indian, living in that world. In the morning, when I put on a suit and go to work, I live in the white man's world. Then there's the world of the Native American Church. My father and I both belong to it. My great-grandfather was one of the men who brought peyote here from the Plains Indians at the end of the last century. People say it goes against our real religion—the Taos religion—but it's no different. It brings you closer to understanding yourself, how you fit into the world."

Contrary to popular belief that peyote is a relatively new intrusion into traditional Taos religion, historical record shows that peyote was in use at Taos Pueblo as early as 1719 and that it was brought from Mexico a century before that. Despite such long usage, peyote has been condemned by conservative leaders who see it as a threat to communally oriented beliefs handed down for centuries. Not too many years ago the council regularly raided peyote meetings, confiscated the blankets of the men, and whipped the more serious offenders. Peyote users have been jailed, fined, and deprived of their property, including land and horses; they have been forbidden to participate in tribal dances and in one known instance were banned from the reservation for a period of years. Users have been accused of trying to integrate peyote into traditional beliefs, a situation which conservatives insist would ultimately destroy the collective nature of the religion. Above all, the tribe must come before everything; Indians are like the spokes of a wheel, but no man may become a wheel himself.

Traditionalists accuse peyote users of directing sacred energy toward individual enlightenment via profane means—in a peyote ceremony, buttons of the peyote root are chewed until holy visions appear and one

Crusita Archuleta has operated a curio shop on the plaza since 1937.

becomes purified. But this is contrary to the traditional way of seeking unity with the higher world. So adverse have conservative leaders remained to peyote that members of the Native American Church are still denied traditional burial, without so much as markers on their graves. They seldom hold high office within the tribe, though one active peyotist was elected governor about forty years ago because of strong political influence. While membership was greater in the early years of the century, according to one Pueblo source, it has declined now to fewer than a hundred participants.

Joe David Marcus is tall, handsome, and broad-shouldered; he wears his hair in a long pony tail and is known as a traditional man even though he lives in Santa Fe, where he has a job, a wife, and a seven-year-old son. He is the son of my old friend Ben Marcus, and like his father, he is a gifted dancer, a man deeply immersed in the spiritual world. I have known him for many years and now, on a lovely fall afternoon, we sit in my studio, talking about what he sees as conflicting forces in his own and Pueblo life.

"What we are is our religion," he says. "That's what my dad believed and what he passed on to me. He'd say, Son, this is the way to believe, this is the way to act, this is what you have to do every single day. No matter where our bodies are, our spirits stay right here, he'd say. Every day we have to feed our spirits just like we feed our bodies. I feel myself get strong just being here, watching the mountains, the sky, a pebble on the ground. Then after a while I feel okay."

He sips at his coffee, his mind far away. There is much of Ben's deep awareness in him, a preoccupation with another world. "I've felt like an old man all my life," he says. "Not in my body, but my mind. I remember when I was small, my sisters used to say, Look at that old man. Because I was always off by myself, thinking about what my dad told me. I used to go out and think all day long about our Indian ways. I always wanted to learn more. I'd just stand there sometimes, looking at the ground, at stones, ants, grasshoppers. I'd see them and I'd see what was beneath them, you know, like things from long ago. I could see real old, old people walking around in moccasins. Maybe there would be deer going by or buffalo. And everything my dad said about those things being a part of what we believed in stayed with me. So when other little boys were running around playing, there I was looking at the ground."

Even now, several years after Ben's death, Joe David Marcus still grieves for his father. He misses his counsel, the way the old man passed on tribal knowledge even when he lay dying in the little second-story apartment where he lived more than sixty years. Even then, people came to him, sitting in silence while the religious leader reminded them of what they had to do when he was gone. But Ben Marcus's last words were not heeded, nor has his high position been filled by any of his kiva brothers.

Joe David shakes his head. "A hundred years ago, everything was falling apart here, just like now. This was a bad time for us, losing a lot of

Miguel Lujan, a tribal elder.

35   Origins

Muriah Martinez.

land and water. Our Indian ways weren't strong then either. A hundred years ago, they thought we wouldn't last, just like now. So a Comanche man gave us peyote and showed us how to use it. A lot of people didn't like it. They thought it went against our Indian religion. But some of the men said, it's good medicine for us, a way to keep strong. So the peyote was a way for us to survive. Still, it took a long time to get accepted."

I ask him if he thinks that peyote will help the tribe again. "The ones who use it the right way, yes. But too much is happening. It's up to the individual now." His broad face is filled with longing for the kind of pure life Ben Marcus used to describe, and which will not come again. "I wake up in the morning and I feel a deep pain inside," he says suddenly. "Something's not right, so I go outside and take a deep breath. I pray while

I'm standing there waiting for the sun to come up. I think how my dad stood on this roof, looking at the mountains, the sky. I want to come back here and stay, raise my son the right way, live the way my father taught me. I want to take the place of my father someday, but maybe I never will."

Here is a man caught between his heart and reality. For Joe David Marcus, as for other members of his tribe, the dichotomy of his people is both terrifying and inevitable. Like 279 other tribes in America today, the Taos face a common dilemma—how to survive, much less endure, within the dominant white culture. A culture alien to their fundamental beliefs, yet essential to their immediate physical survival. A culture that offers much surface reward along with debt, frustration, and loss of self-esteem. Small wonder that the Indian feels confused. What is important? Where is the tribe going? What will happen to children untutored in traditional ways? What sort of an education is needed to achieve unity of heart, body, and mind? How to keep the outside world from battering down their spiritual door when they need tourist dollars for survival?

A backward glance into a living past, preserved through tribal tales, exemplary behavior, ceremonial dances, and the deep teachings of the kivas, offers hope as well as bondage for the Taos people. Is this kiva way not the means by which their grandfathers survived worse times than these? Through sheer perseverance and belief in natural law? During the worst of times, the Taos have always been able to tap into old roots that connect them to a common ancestry as well as to a common destiny. Now old men in all their wisdom do not know what to do. A lingering malaise grips these people, struggling to understand how so many changes came about in so short a time.

And yet. On the first day of every year, just as the sun rises and casts a pale light on the frozen ground, and the ice on the creek begins to break, as many as sixty men emerge from their kivas to perform one of the oldest rituals in their tribe's history—the Turtle Dance, symbol of their emergence from the Underworld. The songs are deeply felt, powerful prayers for survival; the drumbeat explodes from the depths of an ancient faith and reverberates across the icy plaza. A universal affirmation rises with the thin blue smoke from a dozen pueblo chimneys as the Indian people huddle together in common belief and common bondage. It is as if time were momentarily suspended, all wounds healed, and a new, dramatic spirit envelops all. The Turtle Dance penetrates to the very heart of human experience, a natural expression of courage and conviction.

The drama of the Deer Dance, held on Christmas Day during those years when Los Matachines are not performed, is unsurpassed for its drama, beauty, and deep religious significance. During this time of the winter solstice, the *chipuna* or "black eyes" (striped clowns) dart about in subfreezing weather, in and out of two lines of deer dancers headed by two buckskin-clad deer mothers. The *chipuna* shoot miniature arrows from miniature bows at the male dancers wearing freshly slaughtered deer carcasses on their heads; in each hand they hold short sticks which represent the forelegs of the deer. Now and then the *chipuna* sling several of the dancers they have shot over their shoulders and run out of the circle. This drama is repeated over and over again, in a ritual as old as the pueblo itself. At the end of the dance, the *chipuna* place small pieces of raw venison in the mouths of selected Indians, a gesture that seems like a bizarre variation of the Holy Communion ritual practiced by Roman Catholics.

Is the Deer Dance meant to portray the mythological deer of the Taos origin tale, the courageous animal who died so the people could eat? Does it represent a simple hunting story that also honors the deer mothers, symbol of fertility? Did the ancient people who invented these dances so long ago realize the power of transcendence inherent in every step? And thus create a mystery?

An impenetrable veil of secrecy surrounds these sacred dances and other religious rites that pueblo people simply call their "doings." Spiritual survival depends on preservation of this secrecy and on acceptance of eternal truths passed down from one generation to another. Everything is a circle within this complex culture, or rather, a series of concentric circles. If times look bleak, times are bound to improve; if people fall away from their beliefs, they will eventually return because of some deep inner pull as involuntary as birds going south in winter. The end of the cultural world may be at hand, but the Taos believe that their Indian spirit will survive. Somewhere there will be a Tiwa song, somewhere a cloud that speaks a greeting, somewhere a man lifting his arms to the sky just as the sun comes up. And these Indian people, having drifted out from home because of their own weakness, will come back on the umbilical cord that connects them for all time to their homeland.

The basis of Taos Pueblo continuity is as simple as that.

Benito Marcus, grandson of Ben Marcus,
carries on the family's dancing tradition.

Chapter Two

AS LONG AS THE RIVER RUNS CLEAR

Historians have found the first treaty the United States government ever signed with the Indians. It states that the Indians can keep their land "for as long as the river runs clear, the buffalo roam, the grass grows tall, and the mountains stand proud—or ninety days, whichever comes first."

FRANK MARCUS, *Taos Pueblo fire chief, 1987*

O f all the nineteen pueblos along the Rio Grande in New Mexico, Taos is the most stubborn, battle-worn, and secretive, determined to live on its own terms no matter what. Three times in their otherwise peaceful history the Taos have revolted—once against the Spanish, once against the Mexicans, and once against the Americans. In this century, they waged a relentless sixty-year fight against the federal bureaucracy for the return of their sacred Blue Lake. Tenacity, defiance, and an indomitable will have been part of their nature since the beginning. Because of it, they have been tortured, hanged, beaten, stripped of their clothing, starved, made into slaves, traded for horses, and blown to bits by cannonballs. They have suffered every sort of degradation imaginable, yet for nearly four hundred years they have resisted all efforts to rip their Indian spirit from them. Their strength and courage, born of the mountains from which they came, has been tempered by long centuries of adversity that began with the fateful arrival of Coronado's exploratory expedition in 1540; actual settlement did not begin until 1598.

The Spanish entrada marked the end of the classic Pueblo period for the fifty or sixty mud villages in New Mexico. Each of these tribes had a different set of beliefs and rituals; at least eighty mutually unintelligible languages were spoken. For untold centuries the pueblo dwellers had lived in the sun, tending their fields, hunting their animals, raising their families in a never-ending cycle of seasons, birth and death, and ritual. The Spanish descended with a new language, horses, gunpowder, drums, leavened bread, paper, the handshake, surnames, farm animals, new crops, a military government, and a religion that turned the Indian people into slaves. Before the Spanish period was over nearly 250 years later, thousands of Indians had perished; thousands more fled to the desert or the plains rather than be subjected to the tyranny of the Church. During this period of oppression, whole villages disappeared.

Crossing a bridge over Taos Creek.

It is only fair to recall that the Europeans of the sixteenth and early seventeenth centuries were governed by vastly different mores than those we ostensibly live by today. Not only the Spanish and Portuguese, but the English and French, Italians, Russians, and Dutch were gripped by an expansionist fervor that resulted in the colonization and enslavement of whole continents of "native peoples," all in the holy names of religion and trade.

The instrument that helped the Spaniards to conquer the Indians was called the *Requerimiento*, a manifesto that ritualized the imminence of Spanish dominance of New Mexico pueblos. Jointly executed by the crown and the Church in Castile in 1514, the *Requerimiento* asked the natives of the New World to relinquish their lands, lives, and religion to Spain and Holy Mother Church. This document stated that "on account of the multitude that has sprung forth from ... [Adam and Eve] in five thousand years since the world was created, it was necessary that some men should go this way and some another, and that they should be divided into many kingdoms and provinces" under the authority of the Spanish crown, including the poor mud villages along the Rio Grande thought to contain hidden fortunes in gold.

But the *Requerimiento* did not stop there. The final clause of this instrument of conquest bluntly warned: "If you do not do this ... we certify to you that with the help of God we shall forcefully enter into your country and shall make war against you in all ways and manners that we can, and shall subject you to the yoke and obedience of the Church and of their Highnesses. We shall take you and your wives and your children and shall make slaves of them, and as such shall sell and dispose of them as their Highnesses may command; and we shall take away your goods and shall do you all the harm and damage that we can ..."

When the Spanish read this death-dealing document to the bewildered natives, not a word was understood, since it was written and read to the Indians entirely in Spanish. Obligingly, the chieftains made their marks on the parchment, agreeing instantly to become Catholics, taxpayers, and producers of goods and services for the crown. Then the Indians knelt in the dust while the friars planted a cross in the ground and poured holy water over the Indians' heads, absolving them of something called original sin. Before long, the Indians found themselves in a state of moral tutelage, introduced to the cult of the Virgin Mary and to such concepts as Christ, sin, guilt, and redemption. Not an Indian among them had an inkling that through their innocence they would forfeit their traditional identity from then on. Worse, the ancient, sacred land of the Pueblo, an indivisible whole of both physical and spiritual replenishment, was suddenly at the whim of the Spanish fortune seekers.

Immediately an insidious process began that transformed the Taos from natural extensions of mountains, birds, animals, and trees into sad facsimiles of their conquerors. The Taos grudgingly accepted Christ as

A couple poses by the rooftop entrance to their home, circa 1880.
(Smithsonian Institution)

they had for long centuries accepted a holy, atavistic core of worship of all natural beings. Slowly, unconsciously, certain compatible threads of Catholicism were wound round and through their belief system. The cross symbol was similar to one that had been in their kivas for centuries to indicate the four cardinal directions. The Virgin Mary eventually became aligned with Mother Earth and the Taos paraded plaster statues of her through their fields to assure a good harvest; when Mary failed to produce a crop, she was left in the fields, at the mercy of the elements, until she changed her mind. The Pueblo's patron saint, San Geronimo, was accepted because his feast day fell on September 30, which just happened to coincide with the Sun Going South Moon, the traditional time of the Pueblo's harvest celebration. Even today the Feast of San Geronimo

Overleaf: North side, Taos Pueblo, circa 1884. (William Henry Jackson, Colorado Historical Society)

has within it many elements of the natural religion of the Taos, including the foot races and the pole climb. The primordial fertility ritual of the Corn Dance soon was back to back with the feast days of Santa Cruz, San Antonio, San Juan, and Santa Ana during the spring and summer months. Christmas, New Year's, and January 6 legitimized the ancient pagan rituals held for untold centuries on the winter solstice with dances honoring the sacred Turtle, the sacred Deer, and the sacred Buffalo, respectively. Today the continuing performance of these deeply religious dances has nothing to do with their corresponding Christian days of celebration, but remains the reverent expression of spiritual belief by a people who have never let go of their mystical origins.

Other aspects of Catholicism, such as confession, penance, and extreme unction (last rites), were rejected by the Taos. They simply intertwined what they liked about Christianity with a deep and abiding faith in seasons, change, the naturalness of death and regeneration. On their own terms, in the presence of mystery. Rain. Laughter. Ritual dances. Ancient wisdom. The steady expansion of the universe until it circumscribed their own souls.

More than three hundred years after the Spanish arrived with Catholicism, some Pueblo elders still aren't sure what it means. An aged man, Antonio Mirabal, says: "The Catholic religion, I don't understand. It is another language, like being shut up in a dark room. But my own religion, I know just what it means."

To the Spanish conquistadores, the Taos were no longer heathens following baptism, but freshly minted Catholics, bound for heaven and life everlasting. In honor of their salvation, the Spanish gave them appropriate names. Matthew Montoya, a thirty-year-old Pueblo man who would rather be known as Blowing Tree, says: "The Spanish named us after themselves—Montoya, Mondragon, Lujan, Gomez, Archuleta, Martinez, Trujillo, Romero. They were all priests in the old days. Then they gave us other names at baptism. More Spanish names, the names of saints. Geronimo. Juan. Patricio. Pablo. Francisco. You couldn't tell the difference between us and the Mexicans who lived in town, as far as our names went. The old people didn't like it. So they continued to use their Indian names, from then to the present day. There are people who know each other only by their Indian names. If you ask, How's Juan Lujan, they won't know who you mean." (Fewer than two dozen Spanish surnames exist at the Pueblo today. To add to the confusion, there are thirteen families of unrelated Lujans, and a dozen Martinez families, some distantly related. Says eighty-eight-year-old Lorencita Romero, "We're all related, but we don't know each other.") Named, numbered, and accounted for, the Indians soon realized exactly what their new life would be like. When the first church was to be built, friars forced them to drag or to carry on their backs great rocks for the foundation of the building. Huge vigas (crossbeams) were cut high up in the mountains and dragged down. Those who refused

TAOS PUEBLO 48

Matthew Montoya, left, also known as Blowing Tree, is a twentieth-century counterpart of Ventura Mirabal, right, circa 1890. (Denver Public Library, Western History Department)

to work or who lagged behind felt the sting of the whip. Community life was interrupted repeatedly by orders to construct rectories or convents for the friars; dozens of Spaniards pressed into the plaza and forced the Taos to build them homes and furnishings. Factions soon erupted, populations split, converts to Catholicism were rewarded by the hierarchy; dissidents were given lowly jobs, ostracized, sold in Mexico as slaves. Others fled east and west, to join tribes not brutalized by the Church. Elsewhere in the colony, hunger and disease decimated entire Pueblo populations who never recovered. Others were ravaged by slave traders, Navajos, Comanches, or Utes, "heathen" tribes often captured by the Spanish themselves.

Oral history has it that in order to spare their children, the Taos disfigured or maimed them in an effort to keep them from the clutches of such brutality. Other children were hidden in the mountains for years at a time. To protect their women from Spanish bondage, Taos men sold them to their Navajo or Comanche enemies. According to legend, many of these women found their way home years later "because they didn't want to be Navajos anymore."

Further degradation arrived through the encomienda system of tax and tribute. Under coercion, the Indians produced pottery, stockings, shoes, clothing, church objects, and wagons; they gathered salt and wood, hunted deer, buffalo, and elk, all as a form of tax inflicted by the new culture. Loyal followers of the king, called encomenderos, received this tribute twice a year. In return, the encomenderos—the iron-helmeted conquistadores who had claimed the land originally—promised to instruct the natives in the elements of a civilized life, to convert them to the faith, and to protect their villages.

The ongoing production of tribute so fully occupied the Taos that their own daily necessities were forfeited to the demands of Church and crown. There was no time to hunt, to plant their crops, to dance and sing, to observe the ancient rituals of moon and sun. Moreover, they were forbidden to practice their native religion; friars made raids on the kivas and destroyed holy objects they found there. Taos religion was forced underground in order to survive. A deep resentment began to grow there as well as at the other pueblos along the Rio Grande, subject to the same laws and harsh treatment.

Finally, the Taos could stand it no longer. In 1640, they killed their priest and burned the church, an act that caused the whole pueblo to be abandoned for a period of nineteen years (1640–1659) while the Indians hid in the canyons. Forced to build a new church when they returned, the Taos labored on, but they had not forgotten the experience that their fathers had had with the heavy rocks, or the lashings for lagging behind. They pointed to those maimed by torture, the blind, the crippled, the lame. They remembered family members who were sold as slaves, never to be seen again. Taos warriors began to meet secretly in their outlawed kivas to discuss how to free themselves from oppression.

Three hundred years later, every Taos Pueblo man has his version of what happened then. Jerome Sandoval says: "We had every right to revolt. How would you feel if someone came in and told you your religion was no good and forced you into another one, forced you to wear certain clothes, forced you to speak a certain language, build a church, and took your children away? We were helpless at first. If we didn't do what they said, they cut off our food. Some people were whipped, others hanged. The Spanish were very cruel people who came here disguised as religious. We saw through them right away. But there was nothing we could do except go deeper into our religion. My grandfather said what he learned as a boy was how our Indian religion saved us every time the Spanish were going to kill everybody or make them slaves. I guess we learned to be strong against those people."

Church of San Geronimo, 1884.
(William Henry Jackson, Colorado
Historical Society)

Old wounds heal slowly. The Taos have not forgotten the degradation inflicted on them by the Spanish or the loss of much of their land. Even today, people of Spanish descent are derisively referred to as "Mexicans" by the Indians. Marriage with Hispanics is still discouraged and, until recently, was forbidden despite an obvious strain of Spanish blood in Indian features. Citing racial taboos, radical governor Severino Martinez expelled, in 1947, five Indian men married to non-Indian women. Every Taos family can recite real or imagined grievances to keep a smoldering resentment alive. "They stole my land," "they took my water," "they killed

51   As Long As the River Runs Clear

The belfry of the mission church, above, shelled by American troops in 1847, is kept in a state of repair as a reminder of old indignities.

Church of San Geronimo, opposite, dominates the plaza and is the scene of all the tribe's Christian celebrations.

my cattle," are familiar complaints, even though these instances occurred more than two centuries ago. Paradoxically, Hispanics play an important role in Taos Pueblo cemetery ritual. Stemming from long tradition at least two hundred years old, Hispanic men are the only ones permitted to clean the cemetery, to erect new crosses, or to pray orally at gravesites on All Souls Day, November 2. In return, the Indians leave offerings of food at the church for their Hispanic friends, who may have been their enemies not long ago. The political, religious, and economic scene of Taos County is controlled by Hispanics, the same as it was in the eighteenth century. Taos Indians do not seek political office, but figure prominently in the life of the Church, where they serve as fiscales (lay assistants). Because capitalism is not part of Indian consciousness, the

Taos tend to cling to the collective ideal, precluding their rise in the economic sphere.

The great Pueblo Revolt of 1680, which drove the Spanish clear down to what is now El Paso, Texas, originated in the kivas of Taos Pueblo when Popé, a San Juan medicine man with a police court record for killing his son-in-law, came to Taos to devise a way to overthrow the Spaniards. Popé spent four years underground, plotting his revolt, biding his time, dreaming of the day when life would be as it had been long ago. Under Popé's leadership, the Indians joined together in an alliance of more than sixty pueblos, united on so broad a scale for the first and last time in history. Even their old enemies the Apaches and the Navajos joined in the alliance, swooping in from the west. The revolt was planned and kept in the utmost secrecy throughout four years of preparation for war, over a territory covering 40,000 square miles of mountains and desert, among tribes of many different languages and customs, directed toward a simultaneous uprising on a given day. A cord of yucca, knotted to tell the number of days to pass before war was waged against the Spaniards, was sent by the swiftest runners to all the pueblos.

Three days early the fury broke. The Taos Indians were the first to kill all the Spaniards they could find around the pueblo and to demolish the church, smashing to bits the plaster statues of the saints and all the crucifixes. They then swept southward toward Santa Fe. In an orgy of destruction, the great church at Pecos was burned, the immense walls thrown down brick by brick. After a bloody week during which all things Spanish were destroyed—churches, haciendas, and convent schools—more than two thousand Spanish priests, colonists, and their families were driven all the way across the Rio Grande into Mexico. The only whites left were kept as slaves as Popé and his followers set up their own government in Santa Fe, turning the abandoned Palace of the Governors into a quasi-pueblo, complete with drying racks, *hornos* (ovens), and rooms converted into kivas. For twelve turbulent years, the Indians of New Mexico had their vast land to themselves, but their troubles were just beginning. Pueblo tribes weakened by more than a century of Spanish exploitation were unable to defend themselves from persistent attack by Comanches and Utes, as well as by the Navajos and Apaches who had recently been temporary allies. Food became scarce; disease spread; a paralyzing fear settled over the tribes. The irony was that for a hundred and fifty years the Pueblo culture had needed the much-hated Spaniards in order to survive. During the long and precarious absence of their old enemies, some Pueblos yearned for the Spaniards to return.

When Don Diego de Vargas led the Spaniards back to New Mexico in 1692, there was little resistance except, predictably, from Taos. By this time Popé had died and the intertribal council had no heart for further war. A practical alliance soon formed among Spaniards and Pueblos against marauding nomadic tribes, but there were limits to what the Pueblos would take. Although promising a new system based on cooperation and respect, the Spaniards returned with their old biases intact. Indians were still considered vassals of the crown, wretched heathens until baptized and educated by the friars.

Taos Pueblo continued to rebel, even in the face of the determined Vargas and his heavily armed men. The Spaniard found the pueblo deserted each time he rode up the Rio Grande to reclaim it; in desperation he sacked it, hoping to teach the defiant Indians a lesson. Finally, four years after Vargas tried to bend Taos Pueblo to his will, the Indians gave in. They were exhausted from the long ordeal; their fields and animals had fallen to neglect. Moreover, to punish Taos for its role as the instigator of the revolt, Vargas had cut off its food supplies. Many Indians were near starvation.

The return of the Spanish marked the beginning of the end for all pueblos, including Taos. Indian domains were soon turned into Spanish land grants, awarded to loyal followers of the king. Some pueblos found

Overleaf: South side, Taos Pueblo.

their holdings reduced by half, or more. Most Indians did not object at first because most grants were not occupied; they continued to plant their fields and herd their stock, as they always had. Ironically, however, the concept of land ownership was incomprehensible to Indian thinking; Mother Earth could not be owned any more than one could own the sun, the moon, the stars. One did not have to "do" anything with Mother Earth; she was simply there, an elemental Indian concept that was used against them by land-hungry Spaniards, Mexicans, and finally Americans, who believed that every last acre had to be divided up, fenced, and accounted for.

Former Taos Pueblo Governor Santana Romero describes the situation then as told to him by his grandfather: "In the old days, Indians lived to the north, to the south, the east, the west. Nothing but Indians in all directions. First the Mexicans [Spanish] came, wanting a little land. We gave them some. They wanted more. Up there at [Arroyo] Seco they started a farm, a mill, they irrigated their fields and took our water. So we'd shoot them, you see. It was our land, our water.

"We used to have all that land in the mountains, too. We had our gods

Entrance, Taos Pueblo

Frank Marcus, Taos Pueblo fire chief.

up there, our shrines. Every August we'd go up, the same as we do now, to this lake, to that lake, for different reasons. And before long, the Mexicans said, That's our land, too. The Taos don't lie down and give up. They fight. All this time, that's what we've had to do."

But not even Taos Pueblo with all its determination could prevent the inevitable. Land grants were made north and west and south of the pueblo, a steady incursion that lasted more than two hundred and fifty years. By the time Mexico won her independence from Spain in 1821, Taos Pueblo lands had been cut almost in half as Spanish colonists swarmed over the upper Rio Grande Valley. Spanish villages, haciendas, and rancheros sprang up in the valleys, arroyos, and fertile fields where the Indians had hunted and planted for five centuries or more. Disputes erupted over boundaries, irrigation rights, trespassing livestock, and the right of the Indian to protect his land. Time after time the ayuntamiento (magistrate's court) ruled in favor of Hispanic friends or relatives. Time after time the disheartened Taos returned to their old mud village, there to think about what was happening to their fragile universe. Had not the elders foretold such an invasion for centuries?

59   *As Long As the River Runs Clear*

Jerome Sandoval says: "All of this is in our history. We tell it in the kiva, handed down from one generation to another. It's not in any book. We have our history and our prophecy, just like the Hopi. In our Indian religion, we knew the white people would come. We knew we'd see yellow people and black people and brown people before we were through. All the other Indian tribes were described too—the Plains Indians, the Apache, the Navajo, the Hopi, all except the Ute. We didn't have them. That's because they didn't do anything. They were always lazy." To remind themselves of their prophecy, five stones are lined up in the kivas—red, white, black, brown, and yellow—the Indian equivalent of a humanities lesson.

The second great revolt of the Taos Indians was in 1837, when, led by a General "Chopón" of Taos, they joined with San Juan and Santo Domingo in a bloody uprising against the Mexican governor Albino Perez. Perez was hated and feared by all of his poor, uneducated subjects. He levied taxes that the Indians could not pay; he exacted tribute; he also decided against the Indians on nearly every land claims case, favoring the rising elite who were amassing huge empires out of former Indian lands. Led by a group of Taos warriors, the rebel army stormed Santa Fe and routed Perez. The conquerors elected amiable but slow-witted Jose Gonzalez of Taos Pueblo as governor, the first and last time that New Mexico has had an Indian governor. Soon, an aristocrat named Manuel Armijo, supposedly one of the new regime's chief supporters, hurried toward Chihuahua with his troops, met the Mexican army, and brought them back to Santa Fe. Jose Gonzalez's short-lived tenure came to an end when Armijo's guards put a bullet through his head.

The infamous, tragic, and last Taos Revolt of 1847 had its origins in a dispute involving a large portion of Pueblo lands to the east and northeast. French and American fur trappers, pouring into the area from the north country, coveted the rich lode of fur-bearing terrain and pressured the Mexican authorities in Santa Fe for what would be called the Maxwell land grant, stretching more than thirty miles across the mountains. The Indians were outraged. They pleaded before the court, pointing out that these were sacred mountains, streams, and forests put there by the Great Spirit to be treated with reverence. Nonetheless, the grant was awarded to Charles Beaubien and Guadalupe Miranda, cronies of Governor Manuel Armijo, who had killed Jose Gonzalez in cold blood only a few years before.

A silent partner in the Maxwell land grant was alleged to be trader Charles Bent, soon to become the first American territorial governor. Rumors of the role of Bent reached Taos Pueblo. During long winter evenings a faction of disgruntled Indians met in their kivas to discuss what to do about Bent, Maxwell, and Beaubien. Some Pueblo sources say fewer than a dozen Indians were involved in the plot; others say it was not the Taos at all, but men dressed to look like them, war paint, blankets, and all. Indians say that both Mexicans and Americans alike were trying to discredit them in order to get more land. They also point out that the uprising occurred on January 19, 1847, when the Taos are always involved in their "doings," and thus not thinking about such pursuits as murder.

According to Santana Romero, "There was a dance going on the day of the rebellion, one woman and all those men. They heard the soldiers coming. You see, in our old way, we can become coyotes, birds, wolves. A man can become those things just like he was in the first round. So one man became a coyote to warn us. He started to howl over there by the river. Another man turned into a bird and he sat in the tree, calling a warning. That's our way. Braves can be gods, just like we were at first. But everyone was dancing. The shots started coming from town. And the people ran to the church, thinking they would be safe, but the troops opened fire."

More than a dozen accounts have been written about the Taos Revolt of 1847, all describing in lurid detail the scalping and killing of Governor Bent in Taos, along with fourteen others, including a relative of Charles Beaubien. It took two weeks for a company of 350 volunteers to reach Taos Pueblo, armed with rifles and five cannon. In the fear and confusion that followed, more than two hundred Indians, including women and children, took refuge in their church and barricaded themselves inside. With an almost religious fervor, the volunteers assaulted the church for two days and three nights until it finally fell. Mountain man Dick Wootten, recruited for the assault, noted in his journal, "We lighted the fuses, and threw some of these shells into the church with our own hands, in order that they might be sure to explode at the proper time and place."

As Cecelia Lujan of Taos Pueblo heard about it: "When the Americans finished shelling the church, one old woman looked up and she saw through the smoke the statue of the Virgin Mary. Everything else was ruined except that statue. She went up to the altar and took it down. She ran outside with it. The soldiers were waiting. They fired at her as soon as she came out. She ran zigzag all the way to her house. The bullets never touched her. The Virgin was hidden until the new church was built. That old woman saved it."

While troops continued their assault, Indians who remained in the village ran for their lives toward the mountains, pursued by two dozen soldiers on horseback who fired at them from behind, felling fifty-one. Three wounded Indians lay on the ground, bleeding profusely, begging to be shot. Tribal legend has it that these three warriors recovered and became important men and "nothing could ever touch them again."

There is also a legend, discounted by many, but believed by others, that American troops went from house to house, rounding up small boys and killing them. According to this story, when some of the Indian men saw what was happening, they took the boys that were left to the mountains, to keep them safe for the rest of the winter.

Matthew Montoya (Blowing Tree) has his own version of what happened next. "The killing went on for several days," he says. "The Americans ran out of cannonballs, so they used rocks, smoothed off at one end. Pretty soon we realized they meant to kill everyone here. So the five ringleaders came out of hiding. They rode their horses out to where the Americans were and surrendered. It was decided then and there to execute them before a firing squad.

"But the warriors didn't want to die blindfolded in front of a wall. They wanted to die on their horses, riding back and forth. So they dressed themselves up in their finest clothes. Their best buckskin and feathers, their best moccasins. They painted themselves like they were going on a war party. They rode their best horses like it was for a war party, too. Then they went to the plaza. One warrior was at the south end, another at the north. The firing squad was in the middle. At a certain signal they rode

This old woman, reputed to be 117 years old in 1907, witnessed the rebellion of 1847.
(F. J. Francis, Smithsonian Institution)

toward one another and when they got to the middle, the soldiers shot them. They got four men this way. But the fifth one was different. He rode back and forth, back and forth. The bullets just missed him. Finally he stopped and turned his face toward them and he raised up his hands to the sun. Then they shot him. We buried them like warriors, right inside the church."

When the carnage ended, 150 Indians lay dead, seven American soldiers fallen. But the nightmare did not end there. Exhausted Taos warriors were harnessed to wagons and forced to drag dead and injured American soldiers back to town. When one Indian dropped, he was yanked out and shot, and another took his place. One Taos Indian who had escaped the carnage at the Pueblo was shot at point-blank range in the Taos jail by a young dragoon who was never prosecuted. Claims for Indian land soon began to be filed at the Taos County Courthouse; deeds to thousands of acres swiftly exchanged hands, usually for a pittance. Indian water rights were adjudicated to new Anglo settlers who fought with local Hispanics over them. Families moved in and began to graze their herds, irrigate their fields, and plant their crops on former Indian land disputed to the present day.

Meanwhile, the grief-stricken Taos tried to comprehend their shattered world. Says Blowing Tree: "After things quieted down, we went to the authorities and told them what had happened to us. How hundreds of women and children were killed, all innocent. But because we were responsible for the death of the governor and his men, no one would listen to us. They never filled out a report. They said, Well, you started it and that's just too bad what happened. The only thing we could do was tell it in our history."

Taos Pueblo history is unwritten, fiercely guarded by a handful of elders who learned it from their elders, on back to the beginning. Like the origin tales, history varies from family to family, clan to clan; in some families, there is no historical knowledge at all because it was never passed down. Many individuals, who have not had the benefit of traditional instruction, simply invent what they want their listeners to hear. For centuries, the Taos Indians have done just that, as a way of preserving the secret meaning behind their history, legends, and intricate social structure. But within this conflicting framework, an elite group of traditional men guards against exposure of what they believe is the fundamental truth about their tribe.

Frank Marcus says that he learned Taos Pueblo history from half a dozen elders, including his father and grandfathers, and that today only a small core of people still know "the true history." Others know only "a piece of the puzzle," and they spread false stories around. For example, he disputes the popular tale that the Taos hid in the church and were shelled by American troops. He claims that the church was actually empty, that the people tricked the soldiers into thinking they were in the

Overleaf: Pueblo during "quiet time," a period of rest and introspection.

church, while they were safely hidden away in the village. Nor were little boys rounded up, "like something out of the bible." Further, he says that "we didn't ride up and down, waiting for the soldiers to kill us. We never used war paint either. Young people today have seen too many RKO movies."

The question of what is or is not true remains in the hands of a few traditional leaders who are the self-appointed guardians of their tribe's convoluted history. The question of authenticity, in a time when cultural dilution pushes many to the edge of assimilation, is the last vestige of tribal elitism.

Until the early decades of the twentieth century westward expansion was in full swing. Pressure from Washington was on the western states for their vast lands, much of it still owned by Indians. The most striking display of bureaucratic arrogance was the Fall-Bursum Bill of 1921 which, if enacted by Congress, would have stripped the Pueblo Indians of all their land and water rights. Indian activist John Collier and Taos Indian Tony Lujan, by then married to socialite Mabel Dodge, went from pueblo to pueblo, warning them of the impending legislation. The All-Pueblo Council, which had not been active since the rebellion of 1680, sprang to life and waged an all-out national publicity campaign. Members traveled to Washington to oppose the legislation, and to New York and Chicago, where public support was overwhelming. The bill died without so much as a gasp of protest from its supporters.

Even as the campaign to rob the Pueblo people of their land and water was in full swing, another attack was aimed at stifling Pueblo religion. One Indian Affairs commissioner of that period stormed into the Taos Pueblo Council and accused them of being "half animals" and "pagan worshipers" because their religious life centered around Blue Lake. He directed Taos and all the other Pueblo Indians to rid themselves of their heathen religion within a year. He forbade further ceremonial dances or religious rites without his express permission. But the insult did not end there.

Not long after the Fall-Bursum Bill was defeated, the Bureau of Indian Affairs, in a fit of pique, denounced Taos Pueblo for taking its boys out of school for kiva training and ordered the children returned to class. When the council refused, the BIA carted the members off to jail in Santa Fe, several aged men included. Partly because of these and other indignities and partly because of its innate mistrust of all things federal, Taos Pueblo eventually was successful in removing every last BIA official from the village. Law enforcement duties have been assumed by the tribe, while the clinic and the Day School are still administered by the federal agency, a situation that the Indians accept with lingering resentment.

Since the time that New Mexico became part of the United States in

Right: Two Pueblo men and their freshly killed bear, circa 1904. (Kit Carson Foundation, Taos)

Left: Leandro Lucero, a tribal elder.

1847, the pressure by the federal government upon its Indian wards has been relentless. The official objective of the Interior Department was to "Americanize" the Pueblos, spiritually and physically, despite the fact that they were charged with their protection. As early as 1871, the Bureau of Indian Affairs vowed to remove all trace of "Indianness" from its wards, whether it be language, dress, hairstyles, religion, or cultural uniqueness. BIA boarding schools were little more than cultural concentration camps where terrified young Indians, some wrested from their parents at gunpoint, were indoctrinated into the white society. Some Taos Indians were sent as far away as Riverside, California, others to Carlisle, Pennsylvania; but most were packed off to BIA schools in Santa Fe or Albuquerque.

71   *As Long As the River Runs Clear*

Many young Indian students ran away from these quasi-prisons; others pined away and died of their misery. Bureaucrats argued convincingly that the Indian needed to learn to read and write English in order to survive; what they failed to add was that Indians in BIA schools were taught a value system totally at odds with their own time-honored traditions.

Emily Lujan is a shy, graceful woman about eighty years old, though she isn't certain of her age because she never had a birth certificate. In the large, comfortable adobe house she shares with her diabetic husband, Tom, Emily Lujan moves contentedly through the familiar rooms lined with pictures of her family; on one wall hang the required bow, twelve arrows, and a rifle. This is a cheerful house, with blue walls and high ceilings, and a large, sunny kitchen where Emily likes to sit and feel the sun.

"When I was five years old, I went away to boarding school in Albuquerque," she says. "I tell the kids how it used to be, but they only laugh about how we had to march to the cafeteria and to class. Once a week, there was inspection. They looked at our hair, they examined our nails. We couldn't speak our language. If we did, we were sent off by ourselves for an hour. Sometimes girls got their mouths washed out with soap or they got hit, but not me. I always spoke English there. I wanted to learn it.

"We had cooking classes, sewing classes, history, English, arithmetic. We went in September and came home in June. I missed my family, but I carried them in my heart. Sometimes I wanted to run away, it was so hot and dusty there. But then I'd think about how it was here, how the mountains looked, how cool and green it was, and I forgot about how terrible Albuquerque was." With typical Taos Pueblo understatement, Emily Lujan says, "The BIA school didn't hurt us. We learned a lot there. The ones that went crazy were the ones that weren't strong. The rest of us learned to survive, that's all."

The most wrenching ordeal ever faced by the Taos was the long, bitter struggle to regain their sacred Blue Lake, a holy shrine more than 11,000 feet high on the flanks of Wheeler Peak. Every August since time immemorial, the entire tribe, except for the infirm or aged, walks forty miles roundtrip to Blue Lake, there to immerse themselves in the deepest, most secret of all their Indian devotions. This is a time of intense spiritual regeneration, when old feuds are momentarily forgotten, and a cord of commonality ties them to the mysterious lake of their origins. For three days, the Taos rejoice together and at the end of this time, the people emerge cleansed.

No outside person has ever witnessed the holy rituals that occur here, but rumors abound. None other than famed photographer Edward Curtis wrote that the Taos had practiced human sacrifice there for years, throwing into the lake each August one pubescent boy and girl. Salacious writers reported that three days of sex orgies occurred at Blue Lake every summer, with innocent girls becoming pregnant by the score.

Footwear reveals cultural change at the pueblo. Above, women at a powwow wear sandals, sneakers, and blue jeans to dance, unheard of a generation ago. Below: men buy work boots and replace the rubber soles with moccasin soles to keep their "Indian spirit" alive. Left: Beaded moccasins, borrowed from the Plains Indians, are part of every traditional wardrobe.

Perhaps these stories proliferating in the press at that time had something to do with a fateful decision made by President Theodore Roosevelt in 1906. After a hunting trip to the Sangre de Cristos, the old Rough Rider recommended that the spectacular mountain wilderness be added to the National Forest Reserve; 330,000 acres of former Indian land was to be thrown open to increased timber cutting, grazing, and hunting by a stroke of the presidential pen.

Blue Lake was part of this federal land grab, a subject that still stirs the Taos Indians to anger. Sam Romero says: "Nobody came from Washington to tell us. We found out when people were there hunting, fishing, throwing trash around. First they put up fences, then roads. Pretty soon they kept us out. We had to ask permission to use our lake, our land."

Persistently, the Indians fought to have Blue Lake excluded from the national forest system; time after time, they were rebuffed by bureaucrats who waved pages of regulations and restrictions. In desperation, the Taos agreed to the annexation of their sacred area, provided the land would be protected from commercial exploitation and that the Indians' right to the land be respected. Predictably, nothing of the sort happened.

The Forest Service soon issued grazing permits to non-Indians who drove their sheep and cattle onto the virgin grassland of the mountain. Every summer and fall, hordes of fishermen and campers littered the shores of Blue Lake and carved their initials on trees. The Indians complained that hunters left trash and destroyed wildlife, leaving dead animals where they'd fallen. Ignoring these protests, the Forest Service soon began making roads through the wilderness, almost to the lake itself. They built nearby campsites, complete with picnic tables rooted in concrete, deluxe outhouses, and government-green trash barrels. Blue Lake, sacred, cherished, and immortal, was stocked with fish, in a move to increase the lake's value to tourists and campers. Along the magnificent flanks of the mountain, wire fences went up. The sacred river which flows through the village showed visible signs of pollution for the first time in six hundred years. Indians became sick from drinking the same water that had always protected them. The arrogance of the bureaucracy increased, year after year. According to a Department of Agriculture regulation, the Taos were allowed only three days a year for their own use of Blue Lake, provided they notify the Forest Service ten days in advance of their intentions. Even then, the bureaucracy balked at closing the area to the public during August, its peak-use period, when the Indians attempted to worship at their decimated lake as they'd always done.

Essential to Taos Pueblo doctrine is the conviction that what is theirs will never be taken away permanently, whether it be language, land, or an established way of life. For example, they believe that lands now owned by Anglos and Hispanics throughout the valley will someday be returned. The use of language and ritual may be "plowed under," but these cultural seeds will sprout again when needed, in accordance with ancient proph-

Eighteen-year-old James Montoya is a drum-making apprentice. The wrap he wears around his waist indicates he is in kiva training.

ecy. Such confidence breeds a questionable arrogance, but it also establishes a necessary patience. So it was with Blue Lake.

The odds were against the Taos, probably 10 to 1. The government was against them, both the Departments of Agriculture and Interior, including the BIA. Local pressure was for increased exploitation; newspaper editorials pressed for more recreational facilities at Blue Lake at the same time they questioned the Indians' "right" to their homeland. Meanwhile, the Agriculture Department continued to make threats of increased mining and timber cutting, of allowing more grazing and hunting. The Indians were urged to accept the inevitable.

Long accustomed to dealing with adversaries, the Taos fought on, year after year, in their steady, intractable way. They did not budge an inch. In 1933, the exasperated Forest Service offered the Pueblo a fifty-year permit to 30,000 acres of their own mountain, a gratuitous gesture that the

Early Senate hearing on Blue Lake, circa 1965. Left to right: Geronimo Trujillo, Severino Martinez, Dennis Chavez (D–N.M.), and Paul Bernal. (From the collection of Tony Frank Martinez)

Indians quickly recognized for what it was—a way for the bureaucracy to retain control of Indian land while giving the appearance of compromise. Blue Lake and 9,000 sacred acres were not included in this permit, nor were the old restrictions lifted.

The Taos spent the next two decades arguing among themselves about what should be done. In New York, the Indian Defense Association took up the cause on behalf of the Indians and began to lobby Congress for the return of the lake. In 1951, the Indian Claims Commission offered a cash settlement for the land, including the town of Taos; the Indians refused.

The Taos went public with their problems in the late 1950s, enlisting the aid of television, radio, and newspapers across the country; a movie appeared, called *Multiply and Subdue the Earth*, a searing account of the theft and rape of Indian lands across the country, including Blue Lake. The more articulate among the Taos gave lecture tours, to fascinated audiences who signed petitions, wrote letters, and made telephone calls to their congressmen. While the local Taos newspaper and U.S. Senator Clinton Anderson (R–N.M.) stubbornly opposed the return of Blue Lake because they felt that the flow of tourist, mining, and timber dollars to the community was more important, a wave of public support spread throughout the country. The Indians seized their opportunity to gain advantage. A Pueblo delegation, resplendent in ceremonial dress, arrived in Washington. Stately, dignified Querino Romero, five times governor of the Pueblo, went from door to door in his blanket, asking startled Washingtonians to support his cause. The press went wild.

Appearing before a packed session of Congress, the controversial Pueblo governor, Severino Martinez, spoke first, wrapped in his striped blanket, his hair in two long braids. To a hushed crowd he said: "Blue Lake is the most important of all our shrines because it is a part of our life. It is our Indian church. We go there for good reason, like any other people would go to their denomination. Different people go visit and give their humble word to God in any language that they speak. It is the same principle at Blue Lake. We go there and talk to our Great Spirit in our own language and talk to nature and what is going to grow, and ask God Almighty, like anyone else would do." Severino received a standing ovation.

In an emotional session, a bill returning Blue Lake and 45,000 acres to the Taos Indians was passed by the United States Senate by a vote of 70 to 12. On December 15, 1970, President Nixon signed it. A full sixty-four years had been spent on the effort. At Taos Pueblo, on a cold fall day, a joyous celebration erupted. A fever of excitement ran through the village all day and into the night. In every home, a lavish feast was prepared and prayers offered by families, most of whom remembered the efforts of two and three generations to achieve victory. A palpable current of energy and love ran through the people as they danced their hearts out on the plaza. Among them were the leaders who had fought long and hard for the return of Blue Lake: John Reyna, Juan de Jesus Romero, Querino Romero, Frank Marcus, Paul Bernal, and Severino Martinez.

"We knew we would get it back," a joyful Ben Marcus said, decked out in his best Indian finery as he joined in a wild and colorful dance on the plaza. "The old people told me when I was a boy. Every day we prayed. Every day we felt ourselves grow strong." His legs, still strong for a man nearing seventy, were banded at the ankles with bells and his beaded moccasins, which he had made himself long years before, carried him across the packed earth of the plaza. That day Ben Marcus danced with the grace and lightness of his youth and his chiseled face shone with an ageless beauty.

The Pueblo has not joined together in a victory celebration, nor any common effort, since that time.

The realities that face Taos Pueblo as it nears the twenty-first century partly rise from the insidious pressure of the outside world and partly come from within. Mixed messages from the Anglo culture tell the Indian to be "modern," and at the same time it wants him to remain a quaint old relic of a bygone frontier; the tribe issues no clear guidelines either, but rather, simply casts its members adrift in a competitive modern world for which they are ill-prepared.

Instead of providing leadership and instruction, tribal government dedicates itself to maintenance of the status quo via a quasi theocracy rooted in custom, fear, and superstition. Governors, chosen annually by tribal elders, serve so little time that they are unable to implement much-needed economic change or to wreak much havoc either. The governor is not considered the leader of his people, but rather a figurehead whose job it is to deal with the public, the government, and to make decisions about such matters as fines, parking, visitor fees, and family disputes. The real power lies with high religious figures who decide all major aspects of Pueblo life at governor's staff meetings held behind closed doors nearly every night of the week. But as one councilman said, "Nothing really gets

Opposite: Tonita and Avelino Martinez.

done. You have one group opposed to any kind of change, another that wants the tribe to move forward as much as it can."

Taos Pueblo has no constitution, allows no general election or public debate, and prohibits women from serving on the council or holding office. This strict division of roles dates back at least to the time of the Spanish entrada and is common to other pueblos with the exception of Isleta which recently elected a woman governor. When asked whether such a situation could arise at Taos Pueblo, one conservative elder said, "Women are where they belong, where they always belong. They have a job to do. Just like we have a job to do. It's meant to be that way. No change."

Politics at Taos Pueblo is a no-win situation. A governor with a structured agenda is called ambitious; one without goals is considered lazy. Jealousy influences every aspect of Pueblo political life; the general population is seldom satisfied with the current governor, no matter who he is. Rumors and criticism abound during every administration, yet tribal

members are forced to accept whatever decisions are made. Far-sighted governors such as Tony Reyna, Santana Romero, Luis Lujan, Querino Romero, or John Reyna frequently had their ideas shot down by a council composed of men they had known all their lives. That the governor, always selected by elders who form part of the council, is frequently at odds with them, is one of the paradoxes of Pueblo life.

The political system relies heavily on fear and innuendo rather than on cooperation among the people; it rewards those in power and ignores the real needs of the Indians to find jobs, to become better educated, or to have a democratic voice in tribal affairs. "They're in it for themselves" is the common refrain of most Taos Pueblo men who, when appointed to office themselves, are paralyzed by the very system they abhor. The circle is not so much vicious as it is predictable. Office holders become powerful figures for the single year they are in office, influencing all aspects of tribal life.

More than 100,000 visitors a year come to Taos Pueblo, searching for a mystique associated with the West of Edward Curtis, Black Elk, and Frederic Remington. But instead of the noble red man astride his pony, the visitor finds a culture in conflict. On any given summer day, tour buses idle in the heat, belching their filthy exhaust into the plaza. Hundreds of tourists, cameras in hand, surge from one end of the village to the other, sometimes poking into forbidden areas in an effort to find authenticity. The Indians sit in their curio shops, selling bread and trinkets. Some will sing a song or perform a dance—for a price. Old men pose in their blankets against the sun-baked adobe walls—three dollars please. Not until the sun goes down does Taos Pueblo return to itself. Even then, an air of expectation lingers. In another twelve hours, the invasion will start anew.

The culture is an anomaly. By all odds Taos Pueblo should have vanished long ago, squashed by the intransigence of Spanish colonial life. It should have been bent and broken under the weight of papal authority. The Americans should have leveled it in 1847 with cannonballs. Twentieth-century progress should have melted it down into conformity. The people themselves, marrying more and more into outside cultures, should have diluted their blood with indifference by now.

And yet, as stubborn as the sagebrush that dominates their once-lush fields, Taos culture keeps on going, from one generation to the next. Nothing seems able to kill it off. As Ben Marcus said long ago, "We came in with the moon and sun. We'll go out with them, too."

While War Chief Al Lujan plays his drum, Orlando Lujan and Frank Marcus enjoy Frank's granddaughter, Maria Ann Thompson.

81 As Long As the River Runs Clear

Chapter Three THE PEOPLE OF THE SWIFT-COMING RAIN

Corn was our life in the old days. All the colors came from the corn. Yellow for the sun. White for clouds. Blue for sky. Red for earth. Even pink corn, like dawn. Corn was what we lived on, white for posole, yellow for meal, blue for tortillas; red was for the mush we made for the kiva boys. We grew up that way. We never thought we would live any different. Now when we gather corn I say to my sister, Do you remember when we were little girls gathering corn for winter? She says to me, I remember it. I say, Don't let go of it. It's all we have, our memories.

MANUELITA MARCUS, 1987

Manuelita Marcus has lived in this same house for more than sixty years.

Not far from the center of the plaza lives Ramona Marcus, Ben and Manuelita Marcus's oldest niece. She is a shy, durable seventy-three-year-old woman who has lived by herself ever since the death of her sister Carrie several years ago. I knew both these sisters and stopped in often at their spic-and-span three-room house that had been in Carrie's husband's family for centuries. Theirs was a simple life. Ramona chopped the wood. Carrie, a few years older, hauled water from the creek. Sometimes they joined other women of the pueblo to bake bread and to cook for fiestas; sometimes they climbed up the ladder to visit a relative next door, bringing her a loaf of freshly baked bread or a raisin pie they knew she favored. Every day they cleaned the house until it shone; they had no electricity, so they used a hand broom made of rabbit brush to sweep the linoleum floor, to clear away the cobwebs from the vigas brought down from the mountains so many centuries ago, or to reach behind their dependable old wood stove.

The sisters saved table scraps and fed them to a neighbor's pig. In the fall, people brought wild plums and chokecherries, and the two women made jelly. In the spring they went to the place where the wild spinach grew and picked it and spread it out on the oilclothed table to dry. All during the year, the dried spinach made the stews taste better; it gave flavor to venison brought to them by village men after a hunt; it imparted a pungent taste to corn and beans and squash.

Sometimes the sisters walked behind the old village walls to the sacred ground where Carrie's late husband, John Reyna, ran in his youth, up and down the same path where his ancestors had run for centuries, winning nothing except the continuation of a bountiful life. The sisters were always together. Neither woman drove a car, so a relative took them where they had to go, not far, only to a nearby grocery or the clinic, to the

post office or the laundry. Carrie Reyna said she didn't like to be very far from home anyway. When she was young, she went to the Indian School in Santa Fe, where she was on the basketball team and won some trophies. ("But I didn't like it there. They tried to make us into white girls.") She'd been to Oklahoma once. ("Too flat. No trees.") Carrie seldom went to the town of Taos, three miles away, because, as she said, "There's nothing to see." She much preferred her old village, where everything was right there in front of her eyes.

Carrie and Ramona seemed uncomfortable in other people's houses, even though they were invited often. Neither woman ever had children. Carrie had been married a long time to a man she loved; Ramona had been married once in her youth to a man she also loved but he drank too

North side of the pueblo, with the home of Manuelita Marcus at left.

much, so she divorced him. Remembering a time of harmony told to them by their grandmothers, confused by life in the outside world, they walked slowly, purposefully, from one end of the plaza to the other, stopping now and then to speak to relatives. Each familiar face made them remember some incident from long ago and they laughed softly as they spoke of how so-and-so had gone away and come back, of how his sister had married a Mormon and tried to live in Utah, of marriages and deaths and divorces. Everything was a litany, recited each time with greater detail, but with the kind of lilting rhythm to their voices that they once used for the old corn-grinding songs of their grandmothers. Sometimes, in the time-honored privilege of old women, they reprimanded children about their behavior. They loved to complain about the deteriorating conduct of the young, blaming it all on the parents and the loose morality of the times.

The last time I saw Carrie Reyna she told me about the death of her husband, John Reyna, who was governor in 1970, when the Taos got Blue Lake back. "There were other men involved, but it was John who did most of the work," she said. "They never thanked him. It broke his heart." Carrie was a woman of great dignity and reserve, but as she spoke, her eyes filled with tears. She looked not at me or at Ramona but at a picture on the wall of John Reyna posing with President Nixon at the Blue Lake signing. "He was sick at the end," she said. "He'd had a stroke and he couldn't walk. But he said to me, I'm going out the door and up. He meant he was going to die. We said, Can we go with you? He said, No, you stay here. You're going to live a long time. He said it three more times. On the morning he died, I held him in my arms. We looked at one another a long time. Then he said to me in Indian, My love, I am going away. But you will know where I am." She glanced at Ramona, weeping on the bed. "So I know where he is," she said. "I can go to him any time I want." Six months later Carrie Reyna died.

A few months later, Ramona invited me in for coffee and homemade prune pie. The house was as neat and clean as ever, but all traces of Carrie Reyna had been removed, in accordance with tribal custom. No pictures, personal possessions, or mementos are allowed. "She missed her man," Ramona said, pouring coffee from an old enamel pot. "That's all she ever talked about. How good it had been with him. How happy she was and now no more. They had been married forty years. When he died, it was like a light went out inside her. She asked me to come and live with her and I said I would. I cooked for her every day. We went on walks and we talked about how it was when we were just young girls. She talked all the time about how good her man had been to her. And he *was* good, everybody said so. He got a lot of things done. So she'd say, Remember the time John met the president? And remember the time he went to Washington? Then she said she didn't like summer because it reminded her of him. She could see him working in the cornfields or on his horse, riding on a rabbit hunt or up there to Blue Lake. But it was the same thing in the fall. She saw him going deer hunting with his brother or his nephews.

The nights reminded her of him. She remembered his breathing. And the days, too."

Even then the pain of her sister's death was too much for the old woman. We sat side by side on the couch, holding hands in the dim light, saying nothing. Then finally she spoke. "I think she knew her time was coming. The week before, she sat right there and she said, Little sister, I want you to be strong. I want you to stay in this house. And she said again, Little sister, I don't know what's going to happen to me. That weekend she fell down and hit her head. So she just lay there on the couch looking up at that picture of John on the wall. She said, Look at you, up there laughing at us. You went and left us behind. She'd shake her finger at him and get after him, you know, like he could hear. She talked all day to him. Finally I said, If you don't stop talking like that, I'm going to take that picture down and put it away. And she said, Oh, don't do that, little sister, it's all I have.

"Even on the day she died, she talked to him. She said she didn't want to be left behind anymore. She told him that. I was out in the kitchen and I heard her. I said, Do you want to be with your man, sister? And she said she did. That night she got up from the couch and she said, I guess I'll brush my hair, sister. Those were the last words she ever said."

Ramona Marcus sat on her bed, lost in a grief she did not comprehend. No windows exist in this house, so no air circulates. The room was as clammy as a tomb. I half expected to see a shadowy figure in a blanket coming through the skylight, the only means of entry back in the days when there were no doors.

Ramona smoothed her simple cotton dress and dried her eyes. "I still see her," she said. "Out there in the kitchen making coffee. Down by the river getting water. I say, Are you all right, sister? And she says, I'm all right, sister. I know she's happy with him. She wants me to stay here in her house, so I will." She looked at the whitewashed adobe walls and the corner fireplace and the haze of almond-colored light coming through the sky-light. "In our way, you have to bury your grief or the dead person won't have rest. So I try to think about other things. Happy things. Dancing. Blue Lake. Riding my horse. What it was like when I was a girl. Then I look around and I say, It's too late. Everything's changed. How did it change? Where was I? How come I didn't know?"

The changes that Ramona Marcus speaks about began subtly at first, right after World War II, when noticeable shifts in the ancient agricultural pattern began. Up until that time families grew their own food, bartering surplus crops for such staples as coffee, bacon, and lard. For years the Taos had been considered poverty-stricken by government agents sent out to help them raise their standard of living during the early decades of the century when the per capita income was less than $100 a year. But the Indians did not consider themselves poor. "We had a roof over our heads,"

Eighty-eight-year-old Lorencita Romero, also known as "Grandma Little," is only four and a half feet tall.

"we had plenty to eat," or "we were always clothed" are familiar refrains among a people long accustomed to making do. A barter system existed in which a man would bring fifty pounds of corn to the local granary and trade it for fifty pounds of wheat. In spring, he'd "borrow" fifty pounds of seed with which to plant his fields, then return it after harvest. No one kept records; a man's word was enough. Not more than fifty years ago, the Taos still led a bucolic nineteenth-century existence, cut off from the world, exposed to ritual and strict adherence to social and religious law. Their contact with the outside world was usually limited to visits to the town of Taos, attendance at the BIA schools, and what surface knowledge the tourists brought as they passed through. Few Indian families had radios, read newspapers, or provided books for their children to read; recreation was entirely homemade with games, races, and simple toys providing pleasure for Indian children. The government considered such Indians backward; the Taos felt they were merely part of one continuous whole.

Red Shirt Reyna, a fifty-nine-year-old drum maker, remembers his childhood during the early days of the Depression. "We grew everything we ate," he says. "Pigs. Chickens. Vegetables. We hunted for wild meat. We never had any money. Nine of us slept on mats in an adobe house twelve feet by twelve feet. We didn't have any furniture, dishes, or utensils. My mother would just put a big pot of beans or stew on the floor and we'd sit around it, eating with our fingers or a tortilla. We didn't have plates or silverware, not even a chair. We ate good, though. I don't remember ever going to bed hungry, even though it was the Depression.

"My mother sent us to school in shirts made out of flour sacks. They came down to our calves. We wore buckskin leggings, slit up the sides, and moccasins. Our hair was shaved off on top with just two long strands sticking out on either side. I went to school dressed like that. Everyone else was dressed the same. I was fifteen years old before I went to town. We walked there and back, dressed in our funny clothes, speaking hardly any English. Kids looked at us and laughed. Look at those poor, stupid Indians, they said."

Red Shirt is a vibrant, outgoing man who lives alone in a combination shop/living quarters not far from the pueblo entrance. He was married at a young age to a woman who bore him four daughters, then died at the age of thirty-two. One of these daughters died at the pueblo with her husband and small child when a faulty heater emitted deadly carbon monoxide gas. After his wife died, Red Shirt moved to California, where he worked several years in an aircraft factory before returning home to learn from one of his kiva elders the art of drum making, an occupation which has sustained him ever since. The Reyna/Rainer family is one of the foremost at the pueblo, producing some of the first college-educated Taos Indian children. Within their family fold is also a variety of artists, tribal governors, free thinkers, business men and women.

Twenty-two-year-old Jerome Marcus, right, a policeman on the Taos police force, does not wear blanket, braids, or moccasins, yet considers himself part of ancient tradition. Left: Tribal elder Joe Sandoval, also known as Sun Hawk, was never without his blanket, braids, or moccasins. Few younger men still dress in this traditional way.

The People of the Swift-Coming Rain

But it may be too late. One elderly woman whose son is an alcoholic said: "He drinks. It's a shame, but he drinks. The people here drink because they don't feel a part of things anymore. We have seen it coming. Our time was the last. Our grandchildren won't know the things we knew. It's all cars and television now. When we were young, there were story-tellers. They'd go from house to house, telling about the old days. That was the way we learned. No one tells stories anymore. It's all in our heads."

By 1985, only a few farms remained at Taos Pueblo. A handful of persistent men, with the memory of seeds and roots and wet earth still in their minds, cultivated backyard gardens in the same way they always had, without power tools or chemicals. They knew, without the aid of a thermometer, when the temperature of the soil was exactly fifty-five degrees, no more, no less; then they dropped in the seeds, offering a prayer for germination and rain.

Albert Martinez, Jr., still plants the old way, teaching his small son what he knows. One day in May, as he guides the little boy's hand filled with seed corn, he says: "I'll teach him to plant a little bit, year by year. When I was his age, my father taught me. I planted my own rows, then I watered them. When the weeds came up, I learned how to pull them out. I picked the vegetables and gave them to my mother to cook. When he grows up, he'll know everything, like I did from my father and him from his father."

Today, most of the fields of the Taos Indians lie fallow. Behind old corrals, discarded plows, balers, and cultivators rust into memory. In a rash of eerie conformity, more than a hundred identical HUD houses dot these once-productive fields; the houses are sterile, flimsy, and cheaply built, easily assembled from a truckload of prefab materials. Labor is often performed by non-Indians, a fact which makes most Indians livid since many skilled workers live at the village. Lured by payments as low as $38 monthly, residents abandoned their old adobes only to discover that the HUD houses were not all that they expected. Cracks appeared in walls and foundations. Doors did not fit properly. Windows leaked air and water. Vinyl floors buckled. Wood stoves smoked. Upkeep was expensive. The places were hard to heat. Some families attempted to tear out the solar panels and dismantle the Trombe walls, only to be reminded by the government that alterations or additions are prohibited. Other families plunged into debt trying to meet payments for new appliances and furniture. Within a few years, the HUD houses acquired the forlorn look of tract houses everywhere.

Red Shirt Reyna, who built a HUD house just a few yards from his old adobe one, moved into it only to find that he hated it. "There was no feeling to it," he says. "It didn't breathe like the one I was used to. It didn't smell like adobe either." After two weeks in his new house, Red Shirt

Above, Albert Martinez, Jr., teaches his small son, Jaro, to plant corn, then dresses him in a traditional ribbon shirt, right.

moved back to the old familiar one which he built forty years ago with the help of his friends. The whole two-room structure cost less than $500. "It was easy in those days," he says. "You'd go up in the mountains and cut your vigas, haul them down with a horse and wagon. You'd make your own adobes. You bought a few two by fours, some nails, roofing paper, windows. Everyone got together and had a good time. I think I paid those guys two dollars a day, good wages then."

One older Indian woman who refused a government house said: "I guess somebody decided we ought to be modern. Our old adobe houses weren't good enough, so they built us these out of board. It's ruined our fields, our view of the mountains. People have house payments for the first time, not a lot, but it amounts up. The gas and electric bills are high, too. People here can't afford it. What's going to happen when they can't meet their payments?"

No modern intrusion symbolizes the cultural dilemma of Taos Pueblo more dramatically than the utterly lifeless HUD houses. For seven centuries, the Taos have lived and died surrounded by the earth on six sides. Their adobe houses were alive, part of Mother Earth herself, and they protected the tribe from sickness and harm. The houses were strong and durable, cool in summer, warm in winter; they cost almost nothing to build or to maintain. Through his house, the Indian was connected even more deeply to something essential in his spirit. As James Lujan once said, "When you look at these houses of ours, you don't see just a shelter. You see what the earth stands for, the center of our being."

With another hundred prefab houses ready to go up, only a few remaining families will live connected to the center of their being. Like the rest of their pueblo brothers along the Rio Grande, the Taos will soon find themselves living in an atmosphere devoid of any cultural roots, the essential link with the land finally severed.

The death of farming—and its consequences—was not the only cultural shift facing the Pueblo after World War II. Returning veterans, including those from the most conservative families, arrived back at the old village and attempted a coup. The veterans, after three years of combat, were not the same naive men who had grown up inside the pueblo walls in a nineteenth-century environment. They clamored for change within a system that had not changed in seven hundred years. Former farmers, they refused to return to the fields. They became carpenters, plasterers, shopkeepers, and day laborers; some went to trade school or college under the GI bill.

Before long, a revolt took place within the village. Meeting in private homes, the veterans openly criticized what they considered the backward and oppressive ways of the Pueblo. They formed the Marxist-sounding People's Committee, stressing the need for political balance, civic free-

doms, and the convenience of running water and electricity at the village. One man, John Rainer, had organized the Twin Village Improvement Association, in 1939, asking for more representative government, just as the Rainer-backed People's Committee asked for democratic rule in 1949. The uproar generated by these demands split the tribe in two; conservatives lined up against progressives, often within the same family. Soon, the Veterans' Revolt involved most of the town as well as the Bureau of Indian Affairs, as the former soldiers tried to enlist public support for their plans through newspaper articles, letters, and public debate.

While the veterans wanted nothing more than basic freedoms for their people, the power of tradition, factionalism, and autonomy surged over them like a tidal wave. Conservatives, led by tribal council spokesman Severino Martinez, succeeded in diffusing the reform movement through the kinds of pressure long used to hold dissenters in line—fines, confiscation of property, and harassment of the individuals involved. Finally, the revolt died because no popular support could be sustained. Rumors that the changes would adversely affect religious life or that outside influences would prevail swept through the Pueblo and drew the people together behind a wall of impenetrable conservatism. Quietly, the uproar caused by the veterans began to subside. Eventually, the radicals who had led the fight became members of the Pueblo establishment and some of its finest governors.

While major changes, such as a constitution or open elections, were buried under centuries of Pueblo inflexibility, a few minor victories were won. A paved road into the pueblo was completed in 1957 despite vehement objections by the conservative faction, which claimed that the road ran through a sacred area. A community store to break the total dependence of the tribe on local stores was opened by John Rainer, by then a school principal, in 1960 and lasted twenty years. Electricity finally made its way into about a dozen Pueblo homes (outside the village walls) in the late fifties and sparked an armed confrontation with the electric company in 1965. That summer, seven families who had illegally connected underground lines to the main circuit at the Day School were informed that the council had never granted the right-of-way for these lines. When electrical co-op workers came to disconnect the lines they were met by more than two dozen Indians, women and children included, armed with axes, rifles, chains, and clubs.

Electricity remained at the pueblo and extended into some highly disputed areas, particularly a triangle on the north side where the prehistoric remains of the old village are buried. Here the Taos go to pray to their ancestors, for they consider the area the holiest of shrines, a verification of their sacred existence. Tony Frank Martinez, the outspoken tribal administrator, could not support the plan, so he quit his job in protest, saying that he and his family did not want to go to the sacred area to pray with light bulbs shining in their faces. A petition was circulated and

Juanita Dubray, John Suazo's mother, with one of her storyteller dolls.

hundreds signed, but trenches for electrical lines were cut through the holy earth anyway.

Some of the more conservative people claim that when electricity was finally connected to the home of the tribal secretary in this sacred area in 1984, a curse allegedly fell upon the pueblo. One old man fell down and broke his skull. Lightning struck for the first time in memory. Three people fell ill with cancer. Neither the tribal secretary nor his wife could sleep, and eventually moved out of their newly electrified home to one that had no electricity. Many Taos believe that the subsequent problems of the tribe are directly related to this violation of traditional ways.

But another force is at work, and that is the slow deterioration of the village itself. At the beginning of the century, the entire population was required to live inside the pueblo walls, as many as a thousand people on either side of the river. Their irrigated fields, pastures, and summer homes lay beyond the walls; the ancestral village was the center of all ceremonial, family, and community life, just as it is today. By midcentury, only a handful of people lived outside the walls, but this soon changed with the advent of electricity. Suddenly, Indians wanted refrigerators, television sets, and vacuum cleaners, just like everyone else. A building boom began, not seen for five hundred years since the main village was constructed. For the first time in their lives, Taos Indians had running water, and in some cases indoor plumbing. Ancestral homes were closed up, reserved for funerals and special feast days held throughout the year. Only a few families still kept up their old houses the same as before.

Today fewer than a hundred people still live in the old village where the earth was once considered so sacred that even heeled boots were forbidden. Most have chosen to remain in the houses of their ancestors for traditional reasons; for others, economics dictates that they live in a house where there is no rent, telephone, or utility bills. But the pueblo is falling down. There are gaping holes in the ancient adobe walls; grass grows two feet tall on the rooftops; behind the main village whole rooms have already given way. Each rainstorm weakens the fragile old structures; many houses are on the verge of collapse. Not long ago, after every rainstorm, whole families came out and tamped down the rooftops to help harden the clay. Now the rain simply seeps into the old rooms, turning adobe into sand. One man, when I pointed out that the pueblo seemed ready to fall down, said firmly, "It no fall down. Village always survive."

But the venerable old pueblo may not survive. Not only are the outer walls collapsing, but roofs and interior walls are as well. Architects and engineers, brought in by the tribe to assess the damage, predict that unless a massive restoration project is launched immediately, Taos Pueblo will crumble in less than five years. Alarmed by the prognosis, wealthy Chicago businessman Michael O'Shaughnessy gave the Taos an initial grant of $100,000 to help them in their attempt to raise $15,000,000

For Pueblo men and women, chores are ongoing. Above right: hauling water for drinking, cooking, and washing from Taos Creek. Below right: fixing the family car on a Saturday afternoon.

to cover fifteen years of restoration work, training programs, and education. Yet even this goodwill gesture was greeted with considerable suspicion. One woman who lives on the south side said, "He must want something." Another said bitterly, "In the old days everyone got together to help plaster. Even little kids did something. It was a community effort. Now he wants to pay us to do what we used to do for nothing."

The tribally sponsored restoration project, begun under Governor Santana Romero in 1986, continues slowly, for the damage is severe. More than a dozen skilled Indian workers patiently scrape away old walls and replace them with new ones, install fresh vigas, shore up sagging rooftops. In 1988, the governor's office sent out letters to each tribal member, detailing the extent of the damage to the village and citing the need for each family to donate either a hundred adobe bricks or $30 to aid them in their efforts. Only a handful of Indians responded, most of them living elsewhere. Frustrated tribal officials, unable to raise much private money

Pueblo restoration project, begun in 1986, will require another ten years to repair massive damage to old walls and roofs.

or to garner inside support either, are desperately trying to launch a national fund-raising campaign. With its recent nomination as a World Heritage site, along with Machu Picchu, the Taj Mahal, the Grand Canyon, and the Great Wall of China, Taos Pueblo may have the dubious distinction of being the only world-class site that is merely a pile of dirt.

While the village may be falling down, many pueblo-dwelling Indians pay an additional price for trying to live in the way of their ancestors. Burglaries have increased dramatically in fifteen years, forcing people to put locks on their doors and bars at the windows for the first time. Jimmy Cordova, tribal governor in 1987 and a successful businessman, surprised a young man one night trying to rob his store on the plaza. He beat him severely. A few nights later Cordova's store was burned and most of the contents destroyed. Cordova wasted no time. He and his friends mixed adobe, replaced vigas, and replastered the walls. They rebuilt the store,

Cesario Gomez, owner of the Taos Indian Horse Ranch, with his family.

making it larger than the one before. "It's kids," he says. "I've worked hard all my life. They can't drive me out." During his tenure as governor, police protection of those living at the pueblo was stepped up and incidents decreased.

Violence takes other forms, too. Sandi Gomez, a good-natured Anglo woman married to Cesario Gomez, who owns the Taos Pueblo Horse Ranch, reports that eighteen of their prize horses were shot over the last ten years. Once, a bullet was fired through the windshield of their pickup as they drove along a Pueblo road. Former tribal secretary and now fire chief Frank Marcus once raised sheep to help make ends meet, but was put out of business when someone slit their throats one night, then set fire to his haystack. "It's jealousy," he says. "People don't want you to get ahead here. In my father's time, it never happened." Not long after the sheep slaughter, Frank Marcus's corral and barn were burned to the ground. Recently, a young Indian arsonist was caught after a terrifying summer during which he set fire to hundreds of Pueblo acres.

Women living alone in the village especially run the risk of attack, often by their own relatives. One elderly woman was raped and beaten by her intoxicated nephew after he had shoveled snow from her roof. The same man tried to break into the home of an attractive woman in her mid-fifties who is a model for famed Navajo artist R. C. Gorman, a Taos resident. She ran the intruder off with a shotgun.

One afternoon she sat in the living room of her house on the north side of the plaza near the racetrack, nervously glancing from the door to the small, barred window. "Living alone at the pueblo teaches you how to survive," she says. "I don't have a car. No washing machine. No telephone. In the old days, I didn't used to be afraid at night. I'd sit outside in the summer, down by the river. Sometimes we'd even sleep out. You wouldn't do that anymore. Kids are drunk. They're on drugs. You hear about all the violence. Somebody gets stabbed. Somebody else gets decapitated. A woman gets raped. No one does anything about it. Those of us who live here take care of things our own way."

Although tribal police patrol the village day and night and make frequent arrests, few offenders are ever brought to justice. "Oh, he's my relative," most victims say, or, "It's not our way." Restitution is frequently personal, with offenders' families paying hundreds of dollars to alleged victims. A tribal court, presided over by the lieutenant governor, occasionally metes out justice through fines, confiscation of property, and stints in the tribal jail. However, these measures have had little effect in reducing crime or alcoholism rates.

Fear and paranoia have replaced the old bonds of respect and trust among tribal members who live behind locked doors. One elderly Pueblo woman said bitterly, "I don't trust my own family no more." A grandson had stolen all her money from under her mattress, she said, while another pushed her down on the floor when she refused to give him money to buy beer. The night before, vandals had destroyed her outhouse; not long after, her next-door neighbor's adobe oven was smashed to bits. "It was them," she said. "Kids no good no more." Yet despite such hazards the old woman refused to move in with either of her children, preferring to stay in the home she loves. Another elderly woman told about the theft of all her ceremonial shawls by a nephew. "Now there is nothing left to bury me in," she said, weeping at the thought of being buried in a borrowed shawl.

The half-dozen old women who live alone at the pueblo tell me they fear for their lives, yet none will move in with relatives. "It's my home," says a sprightly eighty-one-year-old woman who lives just outside the village walls. She keeps several Dobermans in her yard and a pistol by her bed. One night, hearing a disturbance outside, she got up to find that some young men were carrying off her water pump. "So I took my gun and shot one of them in the foot," says this kindly looking great-grandmother. "Next day I called the clinic to see if anyone had been treated for a gunshot wound to the foot. There hadn't. A couple days later, here came my nephew, his right foot all bandaged. I said to him, You come down my road again, I'm going to shoot you, even if it's broad daylight."

One day shortly after her husband died, the old woman lay ill in bed with a fever. "I heard something in the other room, but I was too sick to get up. When I finally got up, I found they took my husband's big drum, the one he always played. The dogs didn't bark either. So it had to be somebody who comes here all the time. I know it was a nephew."

She stands in her big, bright kitchen, her hands covered with flour because she is baking pies. "I don't think about now. I think about before when we'd lay outside and look up at the stars. We'd watch the moon go by. We'd tell each other stories. You'd hear the men down there singing to the river. Happy times. It's the end of us now. I'm glad I'll only be here a little while."

Old women are not the only ones who feel discouraged by what they see happening at the pueblo. Tony Frank Martinez, the son of six-time pueblo governor Severino Martinez, is an articulate, well-educated man with an M.B.A. from Baylor University. Now in his forties, he works for Taos County administration, the first Taos Indian in history to be hired as a top-level county administrator. In his three-piece Brooks Brothers suit, regimental striped tie, and a contemporary-style haircut, Tony Frank looks like the urban Indian he had become when he was president of his own management consulting firm in Dallas. He seldom attends powwows or participates in traditional Pueblo dances, yet he is deeply committed to traditional kiva ways instilled in him by his famous father.

One afternoon, as he plasters his mother's house at the edge of the village, we talk about what he sees happening to the Pueblo. "There's no center now," he says, "no core, nobody to set an example or be a role model. When I was growing up, we were taught to respect our elders. We called them 'grandmother' and 'grandfather.' Now the ways of the dominant society appeal to young people to such an extent that they're abandoning our traditional ways. It's what the anthropologists call historical discontinuance, when you select the dominant society and follow their way of doing things." He wheels a load of plaster around to the back and starts applying it with a trowel.

"The old ones used to say, When man can do things which were once reserved for the gods, such as going to the moon, the end is very near," he continues. "And now, our ways, our knowledge *are* coming to an end. Some of the young people can't even speak the Taos dialect, so how can they be taught the Taos way of knowledge? When you talk to people about this kind of wisdom, they laugh at you. So it's not passed on except in kivas, and sometimes by parents who have the knowledge which they can impart to their kids."

I ask him if he thinks there's hope for the Pueblo and he says bluntly, "There's only one way to preserve the Indian and that's tourism. We're picturesque, the Indian elite, and furthermore, we live at the center of the spiritual universe. Tourists want to see 'the noble savage' in his native habitat, so why not take their money and let their fantasies run wild?"

With that he climbs down the ladder and begins to mix another batch of stucco plaster, rather than the traditional mud plaster. "See, I do it the easy way. Stucco lasts twenty years and mud plaster only one." He laughs. "It's not going to make us less Indian if we start using stucco, just like I'm not less Indian because I make my living in the white man's world, or cut my hair."

Some younger men, however, are often skeptical about the validity of reservation life, particularly those who have left the Pueblo for an extended period of time. Life in the old mud village is not for them nor for their wives, who want electricity, plumbing, and telephones. To some, the old ways are irrelevant or, even worse, embarrassing indicators of ignorance and superstition. Old men are considered cultural artifacts, to be treated with respect, but not to be taken seriously except in matters of religion.

He is an old man, alone and afraid, who lives in a simple two-room adobe house stripped of most personal things. He is an important man, descended from a long line of kiva leaders and Pueblo governors, powerful voices in the tribe. John Concha, the last surviving uncle of Josephine Marcus on her father's side, was once a farmer, a runner, and a fire fighter, but now he has nothing to do. He sits by the hour beneath the portico of his little house next door to his late brother Eliseo's house, remembering his earlier life. His eyes are pale and unfocused, screened by a pair of thick-lensed glasses that give him the appearance of a large and curious insect. On most days Uncle John waits for someone to come by and visit,

Tony Frank Martinez, former tribal administrator, leaves for work.

for the weather to change, for the tribal homemaker to come and sweep his house, for Josephine to bring his laundry, for the lilacs planted by his wife to bloom, for a break in the monotony. Sometimes, hunched over and quizzical, he paces around his yard, watching the earth, as if he could still see his crops growing. Behind the house his plows and harrows are rusting into uselessness and in the tool shed a heap of discarded tack offers a home to Pueblo mice. Time's spiral draws him in, but the old man resists, at least for this day when I have come with some homemade soup, a candy bar, and the kind of cookies he likes.

John Concha is a small man, not over five feet four, slightly built, yet with the power to swing an ax at the age of eighty-five. His long braids are wrapped around his head like a turban. On his feet he wears a pair of moccasins so old that they have turned black with years of use. I have known the Concha family more than twenty-five years and was particularly close to Eliseo, who died in 1987. Eliseo's wife, Emily, is my Indian mother, and I call her *ka* (mother); for years we have shared a warm and easy relationship punctuated by children, family celebrations, and mutual observations.

On this warm fall day John Concha's rheumy old eyes are fastened on the mountains to the north as if to see in them memories of his youth. He used to be a runner, he says, but this was not like the jogging of today. It was simply a way for a man to be in contact with the earth, to echo its rhythm, to unite flesh with earth, to encourage the earth for the sake of the whole village. "Used to run up there every day," Uncle John says, seeing the winding path he used to take through the low forest of piñon and juniper, up higher to the aspen and ponderosas, across the streams and meadows. "Used to see things. Deer. Elk. Eagles. Foxes. Used to run in the morning before the sun was up. Summer and winter I run. Never got cold. Never got tired. Just run."

John Concha was a farmer most of his life, growing crops of wheat, oats, corn, and alfalfa which he traded in town for coffee, sugar, lard, and bacon. He also raised vegetables that his wife dried along with the meat that he brought home from his hunting trips to the nearby mountains. The old man farmed for other people too, using his three-horse plow. With his horses he got to see as much of the world as he wanted to, as far away as Picuris Pueblo, thirty miles over the mountains, where he farmed for his cousins. (The Picuris are linguistically related to the Taos and are believed by anthropologists to have split off from them in the thirteenth century, when both groups resided in Pot Creek.) Although he has not farmed in twenty years, Uncle John says he still feels the plow in his hands. He misses other essential parts of his life, too.

"Sometimes I see my old horses in my sleep," he says. "See my cornfields, too. The corn is deep. All colors. I see my wife. She used to can everything we ate. Corn. Cherries. Beans. Meat. No food stamps then. No commodities. I'd take my gun, go get a deer or elk. Last all winter. Nothing

Uncle John Concha tries on his traditional blanket.

went to waste. I'd make drum from the hide, leggings, moccasins. She'd make her white boots. We'd sit in the house together in the winter, making things. We had a good life. When the Hunter [Orion] climb out of the sky, we talk about what to plant this year. Corn. Chili. Squash. Beans. But she liked radishes, lettuce, carrots, beets, too. No need to buy seed then. I'd save it up year to year, go around and get what I didn't have. Everybody share. Everybody eat good."

Uncle John's wife died in 1984. The only tangible evidence of his life with her is a faded snapshot on his bureau and a scraggly pot of her geraniums that he keeps in the west window. After years of struggle, Uncle John lost his only son, Robert, to the ravages of alcohol in 1986. His stepdaughter lives in California and visits but once or twice a year. Most of his friends and kiva brothers are gone, too. "No more anything," the old man says ruefully. Behind his thick glasses, his eyes are crossed, un-focused on anything except the immediate present. "Everybody gone. Wife. Son. Eliseo. Used to have horses, cattle. No more. Used to run like the wind. No more. Only thing to do is sit in a rocking chair, smoke a pipe, cigar. Remember everything. What I did. Where I went. What I saw." His memories are like an overcoat; he can take them off or put them on any time he chooses. What he sees today disturbs him. He tells me that his people were once the red-brown color of dirt, but that over the years they faded so that now "they the color of the clouds, like you." He laughs as he says this, a popular Indian joke.

Uncle John talks about peyote and how it came to the Pueblo long ago and why it appealed to him when he was still a young man. "Peyote make you feel good," he says. "But then hippies come along. Ruin everything. In old days, we have meeting up there in the mountains, sing all night, have a big feast." Peyote would make him feel good again if he had some, but no one invites him to meetings anymore.

The old man puts away his drum. His wrinkled old face tightens up in a frown. There is something important on his mind. He tells me that his best friend died a few days ago, and he feels sad. "The earth called to my friend and he went," he says simply. "So pretty soon I go, too. Meet my friend up there in the sky. Meet Eliseo. My wife. My son."

When his friend died the other day, a thunderstorm drenched John Concha's ranch in the mountains. He ran outside to look. There in the clouds a man on horseback suddenly appeared. He recognized his old friend, Uncle John says, and his friend's familiar horse. "But I got no horse, no saddle," he says. "What I gonna ride up there?"

Cesario Gomez is an avid horseman and owner of the Taos Pueblo Horse Ranch.

117 *The People of the Swift-Coming Rain*

Chapter Four THE CORN MOTHER'S DAUGHTERS

Three generations of Taos Pueblo women
include, left to right, Anita Lujan,
Juanita Marcus Turley, Manuelita
Marcus, Pat Michaels.

The role of a Taos Pueblo woman is almost invisible, yet her presence is as powerful as the collective breath of fifty tribal generations. Though she holds no office, makes no political decisions, and seldom argues with men in power, she is the conscience of her people, the essential link between generations, the one who gives courage to those beset by change and uncertainty. A Taos Pueblo woman is the one who bathes her newborn grandchildren in Taos Creek and gives them Indian names; it is she who prepares the dead for burial and works without complaint as she prepares a feast for 500 wedding guests. Hers is an ancient role, stretching back to the time of the tribe's emergence from Blue Lake, when it was up to her to weave stories out of rain. It was she who made food from corn and in the inflexibility of stones found something to remind her of her own destiny. From her lips, whole litanies evolved. Songs grew from tears and laughter. Language exploded beyond mere words. In silence, men watched as the sacred character of woman began to form.

She would be called Ank'ana, Mother; Tomya, Morning Song; Poau, Ripe Corn; Iapatsi, Corn Spring; the incarnation of the sacred Earth Mother herself. She was the daughter of the Father Sun, sister to the Four Brother Winds, mother of the embryo corn. In an old language derived from that time, her name, Woman, was the same as the words for Night, Cold, Long Sleep, and Water.

Daughters of the Water, Daughters of the Long Sleep, women carried their burdens from generation to generation, seeking to fulfill the prophecy of the ancient ones. The voices of the ancestors cried out on the wind, rising and falling like the waves of the sea. And from the bear, the wolf, the deer, the elk, the hawk, and the eagle came other voices as well: You are women, spinners of the life thread, forged from earth and water, the living connection between earth and sky, Sun and Moon. You

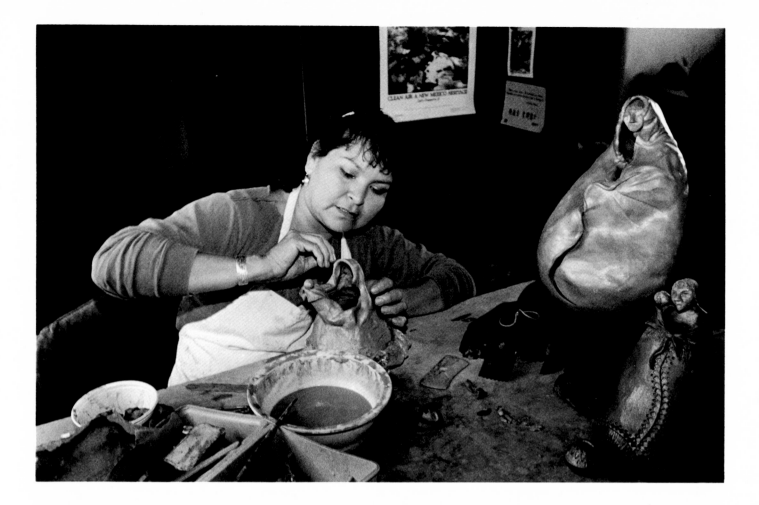

are women, seed carriers, rain bringers, tassels from Mother Earth's sacred corn.

Sharon Reyna.

Taos Pueblo women are the holy and profane manifestations of the eternal Corn Mothers, bearers of the sacred zia maize that originated out of the tiny cinteotl grass, ten chromosomes that divide equally between two new cells. The Corn Mothers are the ovum awaiting the fusion of male pollen; they are representative of fertile Mother Earth, a continuous matriarchal root, enduring to the end of all life. So meaningful is corn to a Taos Pueblo woman that it remains part of her consciousness. Says Sharon Reyna, "Corn is life to us. It's where we came from, deep inside the earth. In spring, when the corn goes in the ground, we think about seeds, new life, beginnings. In the fall, when we pick it, it's like old age. Good-bye for a while. The corn is eaten, the earth rests. Then in spring, the cycle begins again."

Four Corn Dances are held each spring and summer as part of a woman's religious cycle. According to Sharon Reyna, "The Corn Dance reminds us of our life. We have to give thanks to the sun for making the corn grow, the rain for giving out water, the earth for giving the corn a place to grow. It's time for each of us to think about who we are, our place in the village, the ways our ancestors taught us. When you dance you think about where you came from, where you're going. You pray for all the people, for peace, for there to be plenty. The corn is a symbol for all that. Each part of it means something—the stalk going down into the earth, the tassels' pathways from each kernel, the kernels to make seeds to plant next year, the husk that is like a womb. Corn is a symbol of fertility, of life, continuity. It's our connection with Mother Earth."

But for all her mythical origins, the Taos Pueblo woman remains in a bind. She may own property but not acquire material wealth. She may voice opinions, but she must always defer to the man. Her traditional role is to provide a quiet strength and backing to her family, to comfort her husband but not to question his authority in matters of religion, tribal law, or even familial roles. He usually makes the decisions about how to spend money, where to travel, or what position to take in tribal matters. Her role is clearly defined—by the men in her tribe and family. Until a generation

Pueblo royalty, left to right: Mary Romero, Patricia Michaels, and Jan Lujan.

Inez Romero.

A woman carrying a load of sticks stops to chat with a man at the pueblo, circa 1900. (Kit Carson Foundation, Taos)

or so ago, women accepted this situation, but now there are signs of change within the time-honored structure.

Pueblo men seldom do household chores because of strict adherence to the same patriarchal value system that binds their male counterparts together the world over. Widowed Taos Pueblo men will spend their lives eating in restaurants or with relatives rather than learn to cook; they will not run the vacuum cleaner, do laundry, or do dishes, frequently citing religious prohibitions. Yet as economic necessity forces more and more Pueblo women to take jobs outside the home, traditional roles are being redefined. One unemployed Pueblo man takes care of his small daughter while his wife teaches at the Day School. A retired man sits home all day while his wife works for a local art gallery; on her days off she attends to all her household duties even though she is more than seventy years old. Another man who calls himself "liberated" raised their eight children himself while his wife worked in the county welfare office, a situation that arose because, as his wife put it, "He wanted to stay home and I wanted to work, so we traded our roles." A young man shares full responsibility for his baby daughter with his working wife. Other men grudgingly accept the

idea of working wives, though many feel threatened. One middle-aged woman, a cook at a local cafe, says, "When I started to work, Joe (not his real name) started to drink. Pueblo men are having an identity crisis anyway. Here I was threatening his masculinity. So finally he moved out."

A working Pueblo woman is nothing new. As early as 1890, Taos Indian women walked three miles to town to jobs as maids, models, and house-keepers, usually for a pittance. When the bottom fell out of the agri-cultural market in the forties, sending men to the bottle or to relief rolls, women found jobs as far away as Albuquerque and Santa Fe, enduring long separations from their families. After the war, Emily Lujan and her hus-band, Tom, both left the Pueblo to find work in Albuquerque, she as a cook for the BIA boarding school, where she remained for thirty-seven years. "We didn't come back here until we retired," she says. "So I've only been here fifteen years altogether. I have to learn all the old ways before it's too late. But the women who have always lived here look at me and say, You're too old to know what we know. Even when I'm baking bread, I think it's too bad I didn't to do it correctly when I was young. Maybe I don't have time to learn to do it right now."

Not all Pueblo women seek equality or a change in the traditional system. They are happy with life as it is, drawing enormous comfort and reward from their families and simple pleasures such as growing a fine garden, making a pair of beaded moccasins, or building a perfectly shaped adobe oven in their backyard. One such woman is Josephine Marcus, a strikingly beautiful woman in her mid-fifties who maintains a fine balance between her independence and her devotion to her family. She is a quintessential Pueblo woman—wife, mother, grandmother, daughter, teacher of her three small grandchildren, steadfast member of the Catholic Church, and a participant in all of the Pueblo's "doings." She will help prepare an enormous wedding feast, replaster her uncle's house, assist at a church bingo party, do family laundry outdoors in a gas-driven washing machine, or take communion to the sick as part of her day's work. Four days a week the Tribal Homemaker's Program pays her $3.65 an hour to care for her elderly mother, Emily Concha. Before that she cared for her Uncle John Concha and for other members of the tribe, even extending her services to the elderly at Picuris Pueblo. Although her husband, Frank, initially disapproved of Josephine's working, "He got used to it. I told him I was helping the tribe." Frequently critical of those who fail to measure up to traditional Pueblo standards, Josephine remains a source of strength to those around her, reminding them of what is good and positive in their lives. In times of trouble Josephine Marcus prepares food for sick friends or relatives, shuttles them to clinics and to hospitals, and listens to their problems. She is loving, courageous, dogmatic, and not without consider-able humor.

One day Josephine and I are sitting in her dining room talking about the origin of adobe. Josephine says that an Indian woman probably

Plastering with adobe mud is a task as old as the pueblo. Here four women replaster the church, circa 1905. (Kit Carson Foundation, Taos)

thought of it. "The men would have been out hunting," she says, shaping huge bowls of dough into loaves for the upcoming Corn Dance. "They probably lived in tepees then, in the days before horses. Maybe one of the children was playing in the dirt, mixing it with water. And he got in trouble because water was scarce. You had to carry it a long way then, in jars on top of your head. So she probably scolded the little boy and sent him into the house. Then she saw the way the mud was drying. She added some grass. And when it was dried, it was hard like a brick. Maybe she tried it herself and thought, with this mud we could build a house that we wouldn't have to take down. Maybe she was tired of rolling up the tepee and carrying it around. With an adobe house, she wouldn't have to work so hard. It would last a long time. So the women got together and made some bricks and put them together and made walls. Then they put some poles on top and laid some hides on top of that. And there was a house. Other people saw it and wanted one too. So that's how the village probably got started. They knew it was the best material and didn't cost anything. Only

Overleaf: Crucita Romero uses a wheelbarrow to mix her adobe—dirt, water, and straw.

mud and water and straw. After all this time, eight or nine hundred years, it's still the best. I wouldn't want another kind of house." Hers is a simple five-room affair, built by Frank, where they have lived for twenty-five years and raised their children.

Because women are the seed carriers, Josephine says, they were probably the first farmers, too. "Think about it," she says, checking to see if her bread is rising in several dozen pans. This week is a Corn Dance, and a feast will precede it. Tomorrow her daughter, Leticia; her mother, Emily; her daughter-in-law Juana; and I will make great pots of chili, posole, sopa, and beans, traditional Pueblo foods originally introduced by the Spanish. More than two hundred people will be fed, starting at noon.

Josephine Marcus makes fry bread at her family's ranch in the mountains.

Josephine applies an annual coat of adobe plaster to her uncle's house.

"In the very beginning, a woman probably saw a seed lying on the ground," Josephine says thoughtfully. "They wondered what it would do, so they covered it with dirt and pretty soon it sprouted. Squash or beans or corn. Then they made a row, then another row, then a whole field. The men hunted, so there was plenty of game, too. They didn't have to go anywhere for food. It was all right here."

She runs outside to check the heat in her adobe oven by using the time-honored method of holding a piece of straw inside. It ignites immediately, so Josephine decides, without the aid of a thermometer, that the temperature is right. Leticia, Juana, and I start to carry out the pans, working like an assembly line.

"One thing though," she says as she carefully arranges her bread on the flat bottom of the round adobe oven. All the coals have been swept out; the heat comes from what is retained by the adobe itself. "The women turned the farming over to the men at some point." She closes the oven by placing a stop sign over the opening. "Probably they got tired of doing everything—baking, cooking, making adobes, sewing all those clothes of skin, having babies, hauling water. They probably said, It's your turn. The men just picked up hoes and started in." She laughs as she goes inside to prepare the noontime meal—fried chicken, potato salad, bread, Jell-O, coffee, and doughnuts. "So that's how the Taos got to be farmers. You better believe it."

When the bread is done, we sit and eat a loaf fresh from the oven, smearing on thick slabs of butter. Taos Pueblo bread is the best in the world, rich and crusty, never dry or doughy. It's been made for centuries without a recipe, clock, or thermometer. It's never scorched or underdone; Taos Pueblo women simply know how to make it. I ask Josephine the secret of her bread. "Clean feet," she replies.

She is an old woman, graceful and proud, who sits by the hour on a thick cottonwood log, watching the people come and go on the plaza. She says she was born "in the Time of the Wild Strawberries," though she does not

Opposite and above: Pueblo women prepare for a wedding feast. They will bake five hundred loaves of bread without the aid of a recipe, clock, or thermometer.

know the day or year, "maybe nineteen four. I don't care." Not more than five feet tall, with finely chiseled features and a stubborn set to her chin, Marie Mondragon's Indian name is Dancing Lake. The name was given to her by her grandfather "the summer I was born when they went to Blue Lake. He said the water was dancing with the sun, so that became my name—Dancing Lake." In her younger days, Dancing Lake was a famous model for Taos artists of the 1920s, who paid her a few dollars to pose for paintings they later sold for thousands of dollars each. Even today, much of her youthful beauty remains, along with a spirit that age has not diminished.

The old woman's L-shaped house is larger than most, consisting of a living room with a corner fireplace, a bedroom, a narrow kitchen piled high with dirty dishes, and two rooms in front, where she used to have a curio shop, selling bread and trinkets to tourists. The house is high-ceilinged and light; family pictures adorn the walls, including high-school graduation pictures, shots in military uniform, and wedding photos of her grandchildren.

Marie Mondragon has lived in this house more than seventy years, ever since she got married at the age of fifteen to Donaciano Mondragon;

her three children were born in these rooms, delivered by a tribal midwife. Now in her old age Marie wants nothing more than to spend the rest of her days here, though it is becoming more and more difficult for her to remain alone. Ever since Donaciano died, the house has become grimy and cluttered, but Marie refuses a tribal homemaker. "It's my house," she says defiantly. "I have it the way I want." On the day I am there her son Howard tries to coax her to his house several miles away. "I won't go," she tells him. "Why should I?" Howard Mondragon, a patient, rotund man with a crew cut, gives her a withering glance and climbs in his truck. "I never knew anybody more stubborn in my life," he says.

There is no plumbing or electricity in Marie Mondragon's house, just like elsewhere in the pueblo. There are kerosene lamps, a gas stove, and a gas refrigerator crammed full of half-eaten meals brought to her by the tribe's Meals on Wheels program. Drinking water is hauled from the river, reduced to a trickle now in midsummer; children and dogs are playing in the shallow water as I go down to the edge and try to balance myself on the rocks. "We drink this water six, seven hundred years," Marie says as I carry two buckets of water to her kitchen. "Nobody ever get sick except white people like you. The river comes from Blue Lake, so it's sacred." She helps herself to a dipperful; the bottom is thick with silt. "River makes you live a long time," she says delightedly, wiping her chin with her sleeve.

Marie Mondragon was born across the river in a second-story house that's been closed for many years. In fact, it's one of those that's starting to fall down; weeds grow on the rooftop and much of the plaster has fallen off. But the old woman does not see the advanced state of decay of the pueblo. All day long, she sits on her log and watches this house, as if expecting her family to come forth. "It's the oldest house in the village," she says proudly. "My grandfather said it was five hundred years old when he was born." She was the middle child, sometimes called Sarvia or Sarvita, born to Raycita and Josesanto Lujan, a prominent family who owned land, cattle, and horses. "We were rich," she says. "Everyone was jealous of us."

The hot sun beats down on the plaza; the wind whips the dust into whirlwinds that Marie says are her ancestors, returning to see that life is lived properly. She munches on a cookie, dropping a few crumbs on the ground for the "spirit people," ancestors who always seem to be hungry. She pours a few drops of a soft drink on the ground for them, too; at times, Marie pours out a beer for her dead husband, Donaciano, "because he likes it." Inside most Pueblo homes there is a small hole in one corner of the room where food and drink are left for these spirit people; before a meal, families reverently leave an offering.

The old days are not so very far away for Marie Mondragon. At a certain place beyond the river, her family had a summer house. "Wild spinach grows there," she says. "Indian tea. Certain medicines. Plums. Wild cher-

Marie Mondragon, also known as Dancing Lake, gathering wild flowers in the mountains near her home.

ries. Tall grass. We used to plant corn, wheat, squash. We had flowers of every kind, all wild." She points out a place high in the mountains where there is a waterfall. She and her friends used to climb to the top of it, knotting their shawls together to form a rope. There were picnics then, and songs sung because "we were happy in those days." They played traditional games like deer play, leaf ball, and bear old woman. Marie and her sister Annie took over all the family chores after their brother died, riding horses, taking care of cattle, chopping wood, and hauling water for the family.

"Whenever my father would kill a deer, we'd cut it into strips and put it on the [drying] racks. I'd put a cloth over it to keep off the flies. Every day or so, we'd turn the meat over. In a week or two it was done." From their mothers and grandmothers, the sisters learned to make clothing from buckskin; they threshed wheat, using the time-honored method. "Me and my sister fixed up the old mower to a horse and went in and cut the wheat. Just us two, going round and round. We put the wheat in a big pile on the threshing floor, bigger than a house. Then we let the horses in. My sister would be on top of the pile, throwing the wheat down on the ground. The horses would step on it and pretty soon, the wheat was threshed."

There were other traditional jobs as well, among them the grinding of corn at puberty, a ritual still observed by young Pueblo girls. Marie, her bright blue shawl wrapped around her head and shoulders, remembers that time well. "We had to grind corn four days at a time when we were about to become women," she recalls. "We'd sit in this house and grind and grind, with just a stone and a mano [grinding stone]. You weren't supposed to complain or think about how hard it was, only about becoming a woman. The men would go house to house. They'd sing these corn-grinding songs. They'd come to the door and we'd grind to their songs. It made the time go faster."

At the age of eleven Marie was sent off to the BIA boarding school in Santa Fe, where officials gave her an "itchy wool uniform" and cut her long hair. In a drive to sever her ties to her culture, the BIA forbade her to speak her native Tiwa language. "But we sang our old songs at night, lying in bed so they wouldn't hear. We sang to ourselves going to class. We sang in the shower. We never forgot our language, our people. We thought of them all the time, singing the songs." For nine months of the year, Marie and her Indian friends were confined to the school, returning to Taos only for the summer.

Music became the passion of young Dancing Lake, struggling to retain her identity at the BIA school despite frequent punishments that included endless marching up and down the parade grounds and having her mouth washed out with a strong lye soap. She learned to play the piano, practicing during the summer at the home of a woman in Taos where her mother worked as a maid. Marie loved music more than anything in the world. She desperately wanted her own piano and when a trader came through,

offering to sell her father one for two cows, he refused. "He thought I only wanted to look after cows, ride horses, thresh wheat, grind corn. So he told the man he wouldn't give two cows for it, not even one," she says. Even now, the memory hurts. "I didn't say nothing. I just went off to bed and cried myself to sleep."

But the desire to play music never went away. Since Dancing Lake was more adventuresome than most Indian girls her age, she waited until nightfall, when all of the pueblo was fast asleep. Then she sneaked into the pueblo church where there was a piano instead of an organ. There in the dark with the wind whistling through the belfries, the young girl picked out a few tunes, terrified that someone would come and find her.

When Marie was about thirteen years old she met Donaciano Mondragon "in a meadow, under a plum tree. He helped me gather my

Ann Gala in the five-hundred-year-old living room of her pueblo home.

cattle. Brought them all the way into the village." He was a handsome boy with high cheekbones, long black hair that he wore in two braids, and beautiful white teeth. "All the girls were after him, but he chose me," she says, laughing. In those days girls weren't allowed to date, so Donaciano used to court her on horseback.

"He never touched me," Marie says. "You were supposed to wait, so we rode back and forth together, up in the mountains, all around. But I stayed pure." She gazes at the bridge, remembering her courtship on horseback so many years ago.

One night Donaciano, his father, and all his uncles rode to Marie's house on the north side to ask her father for her hand in marriage. She was fifteen years old at the time. "The Mondragon family gave thirty cows for me," she says proudly. "Some boys didn't pay anything. They couldn't afford it." Her fine dark eyes turn to the mountain that she says she has looked at for so long that the shape of it stays in her mind and puts her to sleep at night. "But I married right." Dancing Lake laughs with the rich contentment of old age; when I leave, she is humming one of her old corn-grinding songs, her moccasined feet keeping time in the dusty red earth of the plaza.

Carmelita Romero, Ann Martinez, and Daisy Romero clean wild spinach prior to freezing or drying it for winter use.

Josephine and Frank Marcus are traditional people, active in the Catholic Church, who perform Indian dances nightly all summer long with their children and grandchildren.

Left and opposite: Evelyn Martinez prepares for her wedding to Jerome Marcus. The couple preferred to be married in nontraditional dress.

Rose Albert is a pleasant, articulate woman in her early fifties, the daughter of Luis Lujan, Taos Pueblo governor in 1983, and a highly respected elder who died from cancer in 1985. Rose was married to a Navajo by whom she had five children and is now divorced. She works as a cook at a local restaurant, cares for her children, and for her mother, Crusita. One day, after photographing the second birthday party of her grandson Dale Trujillo, I sit with Rose in the living room of her mother's house. She speaks about the changes at the Pueblo and her concern for her grandchildren.

"I wonder what it will be like for them in forty, fifty years," she says. "When I was little, everyone spoke Indian. Now hardly anyone does. Every man wore a blanket. Now it's only a few old, old men. Men and women wore braids, too. So did kids. It was part of being Indian, you never cut your hair. Take clothing. We used to make all our own, out of flour sacks or whatever material was handy. Leggings were made of deerskin. They were soft and never wore out. You handed them down, son to son. All the kids wore moccasins. Now maybe only a few old men do. And that was related to our religion, too, having the hide of a deer next to your skin.

"I expect I'll live to see the day when there's no one left in the village. We'll use our village houses when somebody dies or for fiestas. But you won't see anybody living there without electricity or water. I remember when we used to. But I wouldn't want to go back and live that way again. It's too hard. Women today have other things to do. They work in town. Or they want to take it easy, have television, a phone. Ask people why they live there, they'll say it's for religious reasons. But probably it has something to do with money, too."

Rose's father, Luis Lujan, was one of the last great men of his generation, imparting the ancient teachings to his family and to his people, just as young kiva men will someday do with their own children. Rose Albert, cleaning up after the party, says, "My dad was very strict. But he was fair,

too. He saw what was going to happen and he tried to warn us. He said, Someday you'll have to do the work of a man." She laughs. "Well, it's true. Last year Angie [her twenty-four-year-old daughter] and I had to take the roof off our old house in the pueblo. The roof was leaking down into the room below. We did it ourselves, no man around to help us. We took all the dirt off and threw it on the roof next door. It was hard work. My arms ached for a week. We finally got down to the paper and replaced it and put boards over that. Then we put the dirt back. Maybe a ton. All that work and just the two of us and two shovels. It took two women to do the work of half a man. But we got it done in two days.

"Now more boards are rotting in another place. So we have to take the roof off again. In the old days, a woman never would have done this kind of work. It would have been done by a man. We're changing in the work we do—plastering, chopping wood, hauling water, fixing roofs. A lot of us Pueblo women are divorced, so we have responsibility for our children, too. You tell me, with all this work, who has time to dance and bake bread and be a traditional Indian woman, too?"

For modern Pueblo women, who more and more are assuming the role of breadwinners, the dilemma is indeed how to maintain their traditional role within the community they love at the same time that they recognize the need to forge a separate identity of their own. This issue divides the highly conservative Pueblo, where divorce is frowned upon, illegitimacy and premarital sex are considered taboo, and women are expected to conform to tribal standards set by men. Fifty-one-year-old Tommy Martinez accurately described the staunchly traditional attitude of his tribe when he said: "Women are the carriers of the family. That's their job. We're the carriers of the religion. That's our job."

But such arbitrary lines conflict with the realities of everyday pueblo life. Forty-year-old Crusita Lujan has to juggle three roles: a teacher's aide at the Day School, a wife and mother of four children, as well as her tribal responsibilities. The daughter of a beloved pueblo leader, Quirino Romero, and his wife, Daisy, Crusita received a traditional education at the pueblo. "My parents encouraged me to be who I was," she says. Her husband, silversmith Albino Lujan, himself the son of a prominent pueblo leader, often watches their baby daughter, Shannon, so that Crusita can work or attend classes. Someday she hopes to become a full-fledged teacher. "Al really supports me," she says. "So do the kids. Otherwise I'd never make it."

Other Taos Pueblo women show their individuality differently, such as thirty-five-year-old Sharon Reyna, a gifted potter who has won numerous awards for her unusual designs in clay. A graduate of the prestigious Institute of American Indian Art in Santa Fe, she is also the divorced mother of two teenage boys and is struggling to make it on her own as an artist in Santa Fe. Some members of her own family have criticized her for her divorce and for her decision to have a career, but as she says, "I tell

Pueblo women replaster a family home every year, hauling heavy buckets of wet plaster up the ladder themselves.

them it's my life. I have the right to do what I want. Now, in my mother's time, they would have run her out of the village for saying that. We had strict, strict, strict rules for men and women both until just a little while ago. Maybe television did it. Maybe when everybody got a car. Maybe it was the fact that we all go to school now. The men are still trying to control us, but they can't anymore."

On this particular day Sharon and I are off to the Indian Art and Trade Fair at San Ildefonso, about forty miles south. For years she has been considered something of an upstart at the pueblo for her unorthodox views. A few years ago, when everyone was signing up for a typical HUD house, Sharon decided to build a *round* house, the first such one on the reservation. Tribal members were scandalized, accusing Sharon of building a Navajo hogan. "A round house was what I wanted," she insists. "Everything is round in nature—the sun, the moon, a bird's nest, a pebble dropped into the water. I like my round house." When she was divorced

Children playing in their backyard, left to right: Leona Mirabal, Muriah Martinez, Dawn Star Looking Elk, and Donna Martinez.

from Joseph Lujan, Sharon resumed her maiden name of Reyna, and caused an uproar. "People thought it was terrible," she says. "Like I was putting Joe down or making it seem like my boys were bastards. I wanted my own name, but there are people who still won't call me anything but Lujan."

As she drives along the winding road from Taos through the canyon, she becomes suddenly quiet and reflective. "Changes like these are just the tip of the iceberg. It really goes a whole lot deeper to the structure itself. We're losing our language, our dances, a lot of the old stories. Kids aren't picking up the culture. They're not interested in it. Men are sitting there confused, wondering if even the kivas will last. Women are getting ready for the day when they have to do everything. Many of them are already. It's just a matter of time."

Down near Pilar two golden eagles wheel overhead above the cliffs. Sharon slows her truck to a halt and we watch them for several minutes, marveling at their grace and beauty. "I've been thinking about history a lot," she says, heading down the road again. "What it must have been like here before the white man came. Our land. Who thought about building a pueblo five stories high? The way they must have danced? How they hunted then, with just their bows and arrows? Everybody went everywhere on foot. When visitors came, they stayed a month, a year. There were dances and feasts and, every day, beauty all around, everywhere they looked. According to our stories, there were no wars, no famines, no diseases. People lived a long time. It must have been happy then. There was a government within the tribe. There were laws. And our religion was just as strong then as it is now or we wouldn't have lasted so long. Then I think about when the Spaniards came, how the people must have resisted that religion. I think about the ones who were killed because they resisted, how finally it was decided to accept it. How painful it must have been seeing the land where they'd hunted and their grandfathers had hunted for hundreds and hundreds of years all of a sudden belonging to the Spanish. Some of these people were my ancestors. My relatives still talk about it. You see, our history is something we live with and refer to every single day. It's a way for us to survive."

Deeply tied to tradition at the same time she cherishes her hard-won freedom, Sharon Reyna moved into the old village a few years ago, just to have the experience. She cleaned out her grandmother's old two-room house and moved in with her bed, a chest of drawers, a table, and two chairs. Like everyone else who lives the old way, Sharon hauled her water from the river, chopped her own wood, used an outhouse, and adjusted to life without any conveniences whatsoever.

"I tried to live my life in the village because I liked it," she says. "It made me feel connected to my ancestors and the things I was telling you about. Well, I soon found out there is no privacy. I'd be walking from my car to the door, carrying groceries, and this tourist would stop me and say, Do you mind if I take your picture? And there I'd be, this time carrying my dirty wash to the laundry. What's it like here, they'd say, and I thought to myself, Even if I told you, you wouldn't believe me. There was never a day when some tourist wasn't there when I went in or out the door.

"One day I was taking a bath in the living room and this man walked in the door. He thought it was a curio shop. My sister yelled at him to get out. So after that I thought, Who needs it? I moved away from the village. I think everyone will move away after a while. They'll get sick of all the tourists and they'll get tired of hauling water. The young people especially. When they grow up, they won't want to live like their grandparents. They'll want modern houses and electricity and plumbing. It's part of life.

"In a hundred years Taos Pueblo will look like Mesa Verde. All ruins. When my sons are old men and they bring their grandchildren to the village, one of them will say, Look, that's where our great-grandmom used to live. And it'll be like looking at a relic. But you know what? The tourists will still be there taking pictures of my great-grandkids looking at the house where I used to live."

Juanita Dubray is neither a liberated Pueblo woman nor one tied to strict traditional ways either. At fifty-six, she has found her own niche at the pueblo itself, living in a family compound that consists of her brother Ralph Suazo, a wood carver, and her sister Geronima Track, a potter. The family is strong and supportive, artistic and outspoken, with nieces, nephews, children, and grandchildren coming and going all day long. Juanita's son, John Suazo, is a gifted sculptor with a national following; her daughter died several years ago in a motorcycle accident. Other tragedies have befallen this family, such as the brutal murder of Abran Track, Geronima's only son, and a promising artist in his own right.

"You can't take it when your own children die," says Juanita Dubray one day, putting the finishing touches on a storyteller doll which she will sell in Santa Fe. She lives from sale to sale, but has thus far refused any government assistance, preferring to do it on her own. "When my daughter died, the bottom fell out of my life. I thought I would never be able to make a pot again. But she was there, telling me, You can do it, Mom. I still had quite a bit of the clay left that she had gotten for me before she died. So I got it out and I started to work again. And pretty soon the pot took on its own form, one I hadn't even thought of, and I realized it was Nanette right there in the clay. So I've been making pots and storyteller dolls ever since, as a way of staying in touch with her."

She puts the doll aside and stands on the patio of the house that John built for her. It is clean, neat, and airy, with a view toward the village a mile or so down the road. She pulls up a chair and sits down, turning a pot over

These two young women photographed along Taos Creek by Edward Curtis in 1905 (Smithsonian Institution) bear little resemblance to teenager Zoe Romero, photographed in 1986.

and over in her hands. "The pottery is like your children," she says. "You don't make demands on it. You try and give it something and it gives something back to you. Something has to happen between you and the clay. First, you have to let go of something inside yourself. If you keep it in, the pottery will be no good. Then there's a point at which the clay comes alive. You can feel it in your fingers, like a tingle. The texture changes. At this point, something from you goes into the clay. The clay gives something out, so the piece will have a spirit to it. And there will be something good in your house every day." She looks toward the VW bug that belonged to her daughter. "So now I'm not sad about my daughter anymore. I look at this pot or that doll and I say, Thank you."

149   *The Corn Mother's Daughters*

A few Taos women have managed to combine all their roles successfully, and they do it without complaining. Clara Martinez has worked in a local art gallery for more than thirty years in addition to rearing a family of four sons. Her husband, Albert, was a farmer, a rodeo hand, a drum maker, and a worker for the Forest Service, but has never held a steady job. Even at the age of seventy-three, Clara still works three days a week and admits she gets tired from so many long hours on her feet. On her days off, she cleans her large house, shops for groceries, does the laundry, and in summer tends a large garden in the back of her house.

"I ask God to help me and He does," she says, standing in her large kitchen making fry bread one Saturday afternoon. "He answers my prayers even when I think things will never turn out right. I just go on, that's all." She drops a wad of dough into a pan of grease and it sizzles and rises

"The Grandmothers" (children's helpers) at a Headstart graduation, left to right: Anita Lujan, Tonita M. Lujan, Manuelita Marcus, and Mrs. Teresino Jiron.

into a puffy ball the size of a salad plate. "I worked hard all my life. I had to. We never had much money, no luxuries, not even water or electricity. I hauled water from the river when I was five years old, I swept the roof, I gathered wood, I dried spinach, meat, fruit. I never thought of it as hardship. It was just what we had to do. The tiniest girl knows she has to do certain things, help her family, take care of the house, learn the Indian way. But every day you see the white man's ways getting closer. When my granddaughters are my age I wonder what they'll pass on to *their* granddaughters."

A younger generation of women sees a different situation than the one described by Clara Martinez. "It's not realistic, thinking women ought to be at home taking care of kids," says Cynthia Bernal Pemberton, a bright young woman with a college degree in education. "Men can't get jobs, so the women have to go out and work to support the family. But the men resent it." Divorced, with three young children to support, she works in the tribal office five days a week and does beadwork in her spare time. "So they get drunk, beat up their wives and children. You can kick them out or take it. If you take it, you're dead. If you kick them out, people will shun you. They'll say, What's the matter with her? She couldn't keep her man." For Cynthia, family, work, and participating in tribal events form the central theme of her life. "I don't care if I never get married again," she says. "I have a lot of support right here."

In Taos Pueblo, now, as always, the old ways prevail and there is no sign of women's liberation. Nor do most Pueblo women want to be liberated, citing their need for security in traditional values. One young woman, who asked that her name not be used, said, "I've got a college degree. I've dated white men. I've lived in cities. For a while I tried to shake it off, you know, what everyone says is Pueblo repression. But what we have to put up with here is not as bad as what you white people have to put up with out there. We have roots, and you don't. We have each other, and you don't. So every time I get fed up with the pettiness here, I go away for a while. Then I come home and see the pueblo for what it really is. For me, it's a buffer zone."

A Pueblo woman possesses an equanimity derived from a close network of village, family, and her own place in the kiva religion. She knows who she is from the inside out, and she does not require reassurance. For her, the laughter of children, the love of a man, and acceptance by her family is proof enough of a life well-lived. A Pueblo woman seldom complains; she merely survives, bound to tradition all the days of her life. The village, suspicious, weary, and inexorable, stifles her vision and limits her horizon at the same time it offers protection and continuity. Above all, a Pueblo woman knows she is not alone. Again and again, her Pueblo sisters join together in a never-ending round of weddings, funerals, kiva graduations, feast days, and baptisms. These are the ties that bind one woman to another, one generation to the one preceding, the present-day village to the memory of one in a long-ago time.

On the north side of the village, Anita Lujan has rejoiced in a traditional life for eighty-seven years. She is an almost painfully shy widow who has lived inside the village walls all her life, most of it the same two-room house she now occupies with an unmarried nephew. In all this time, she has never gone very far from home, preferring to reflect on the mystery of the mountains, the river, and the eagles there at the village.

Anita Lujan has a finely featured face, formed by eight decades of observation and reflection; she wears long braids, a shawl, and moccasins. She is uncomfortable speaking English and when she talks to those in the village, it is always in Tiwa. On most days, Anita Lujan says nothing at all, but today I have brought her some pictures of Pat Michaels, her favorite niece. In return, Anita gives me a string of ceremonial corn that her nephew grew in his field behind the village. She begins to talk about what she remembers.

"I came over here [to the north side] in 1919 when I got married," she says in a low voice. "I was a Lucero. We lived on the south side. After I got married, I never went back. I stayed here with my husband until he passed on in 1977. No, we didn't have any children. Every day we walked around, looked at the sky, mountains, the river. He used to say, We have the best place here, so why go away? He'd go to his fields, sometimes did a little work in town. We weren't rich, but we never thought we were poor. We had this little house, everything good was here, we had enough to eat.

"All the women were alike then, too. Maybe one, two go out to work. The rest stay here, cook, wash, clean, make clothes, like Indian women supposed to do. Now they want to go out to work, have cars, electricity, clothes. I say, what for? They cut their hair like white women, put in curl. When they dance [the Corn Dance] I won't go. Not like it used to be. They talk and laugh, speak English, wear short hair.

"Now all the people come past my door. The dust blows in, so I shut the door. So many people from all over. Sometimes they come right in. They say, You live here? Can we take your picture? What you got to sell?" She shakes her head sadly. Clearly, life is not what she wants it to be. "Me and my sister and some other old ladies are all that's left in the village. When we go, nobody will live here. It's too hard. They want an easy life. They no want to haul water, chop wood, do things the hard way. Maybe I'll be the last one here. I was eighty-seven in May. I won't last long. I'll take my memories with me. I don't want to leave anything behind."

For all the bitterness and fear that exists among lonely old women at the pueblo, there is often hope, grace, and a sense of history among those who are younger. One such woman is twenty-one-year-old Patricia Michaels, free-spirited, beautiful, and deeply immersed in a burgeoning

Manuelita Marcus fixes the hair of her granddaughter, Pat Michaels.

153 The Corn Mother's Daughters

Patricia Michaels.

career as a fashion designer in Santa Fe. A favorite granddaughter of Ben Marcus, a grandniece of Anita Lujan, the daughter of an Indian dancer mother and a Polish father, Pat has grown from a wide-eyed toddler filled with curiosity to a poised and mature woman totally committed to her work, her family, and her tribe. Patricia was Miss Indian New Mexico in 1987, representing the pueblo at endless dinners, dances, luncheons, and fairs throughout the state, always graceful, dignified, and controlled. All that year small girls followed Pat Michaels around and she would bend down and listen to them, then tell them to follow the Indian way no matter how difficult it was. When Taos Pueblo gave her an honorary dance in the spring, Pat Michaels put on her silver and turquoise crown, her high-topped white boots, and a manta her mother, Juanita Turley, made especially for the occasion, and greeted a throng of dignitaries and well-wishers before she danced with the same exquisite grace that seems to run in the Marcus family. For once, not a word of jealousy or criticism was spoken by her tribespeople.

Early one morning, before the tourists arrive, Pat Michaels and I sit on the roof of Manuelita Marcus's house, where Pat is currently living. She is dressed in a Corn Dance manta for a photography session later on; her large, lustrous eyes are on the mountains, just the way Ben Marcus's used to be.

"I decided to come back here and live with my grandmother for a while," she says, her shiny black hair blowing in the wind. "I want to feel the way it used to be here. I think of all the generations before me, thousands and thousands of years, who slept here. I think of the dances and ceremonies they had. I think of the mountain reminding them to keep strong. I think about the men going out to hunt in the mountains and the women picking wild plums in the fall. I think about the feasts they had, with everyone preparing food in these same old houses for hundreds and hundreds of years. I wonder what it was like here then. I wonder what my ancestors looked like. Sometimes, if I try, I can see them coming across the plaza, dressed the way they used to. I can see the plaza filled with wagons, too, and men like my grandfather planting their fields up there in the mountains. I wish I lived back then, to see what it was like. I say to myself, I'm part of all this. I'm not going to let anybody down. When I was small, my grandfather said to me, Don't let people tell you what to do. Be who you are."

Manuelita Marcus comes out and stands in the sun, the way she's done every day for the sixty years she's lived in this house with her family, nine children plus herself and Ben crammed into two small rooms. They slept and ate on the dirt floor and they kept warm with a small corner fireplace until Ben bought an iron cookstove for his wife. This is a house of memory, five centuries of it, a house where the dust of ancestors sifts down from vigas raised into place long before Columbus. The house becomes her now. She's been here so long that she's worn her own pattern into the linoleum floor and the old mud rooftop where she stands the way Ben used to, watching the mountains and the ever-changing sky.

The old woman seems to know what I'm thinking. "Ben stood right here," she says. "Saw everything." A woman of few words, Manuelita communicates simply by being who she is, a tiny woman not even five feet tall, who plants herself like a great, round tree. Self-consciously, she embraces her granddaughter and the two talk excitedly in Tiwa. Then the old woman expertly fixes Pat's hair in a traditional Taos Pueblo bun as the young woman sits in a chair next to the woodpile. In two or three minutes she is finished and she steps back, admiring Patricia's loveliness.

"She turned out good," she says. "Ben knows she turned out good." Manuelita looks the same as she did when I first met her in 1961, with her homemade cotton dress and her moccasins, except now there are white streaks in her hair and her round shoulders are bending toward the earth. The death of Ben, while it extinguished some part of her old fire, has awakened in her a sense of obligation toward finishing what he began to teach his grandchildren.

"I am learning so much from her," Pat says, squeezing her hand. "Things I never knew. At night, she lies in her bed and I lie in mine and she tells me stories in the dark. No matter where I am, I'll always come back here. The mountains are a source for us, while the village is the center. When you come inside, there is peace. When you wake up in the morning you feel good. Coming into the village means going back in time. You walk where they walked. You see the same sky, the same mountains. Probably you say the same words, but the language was different then. Here in the plaza is where they had their dances, the same as we do now. The kivas are the same kivas. The wall is the same wall. The river is the same river. Living here you feel connected to all that."

I am but a footprint on the earth,
A wing against the sky,
A shadow in the water,
A voice beneath the fire.
I am one footstep going on.

Bibliography

Adams, Ansel, and Mary Austin. *Taos Pueblo*. Boston: New York Graphic Society, 1977.

Bodine, John J. "Taos Pueblo." Master's thesis, Tulane University, 1967.

Campbell, Joseph. *The Hero with a Thousand Faces*. Princeton: Princeton University Press, 1968.

Churchill, Ward, ed. *Marxism and Native Americans*. Boston: South End Press, 1983.

Collier, John. *Indians of the Americas: The Long Hope*. New York: Mentor, 1947.

———. *On the Gleaming Way*. Chicago: Swallow Press, 1962.

Crane, Leo. *Desert Drums: The Pueblo Indians of New Mexico, 1540–1928*. Boston: Little, Brown, 1928.

Curtis, Edward S. *The North American Indian*. Vol. 16. Norwood, Mass.: Plimpton Press, 1926.

De Buys, William. *Enchantment and Exploitation: The Life and Hard Times of a New Mexico Mountain Range*. Albuquerque: University of New Mexico Press, 1985.

Deloria, Vine, Jr. *Custer Died for Your Sins: An Indian Manifesto*. New York: Macmillan, 1969.

———. *God Is Red*. New York: Grosset and Dunlap, 1973.

———, and Clifford Lytle. *The Nations Within: The Past and Future of American Indian Sovereignty*. New York: Pantheon Books, 1984.

Dozier, Edward P. *The Pueblo Indians of North America*. New York: Holt, Rinehart and Winston, 1970.

Dutton, Bertha P. *Sun Father's Way*. Albuquerque: University of New Mexico Press, 1963.

Erdoes, Richard. *The Pueblo Indians*. New York: Funk and Wagnall, 1967.

Fenton, William N. *Factionalism at Taos Pueblo, New Mexico*. Washington, D.C.: Bureau of Ethnography, 1957.

Garrard, Lewis H. *Wah-to-Yah and the Taos Trail*. Norman: University of Oklahoma Press, 1955.

Gilpin, Laura. *The Enduring Navajo*. Austin and London: University of Texas Press, 1968.

———. *The Pueblos: A Camera Chronicle*. New York: Hastings House, 1941.

Grant, Blanche C. *The Taos Indians*. Glorieta, N.M.: Rio Grande Press, 1976.

Hackett, C. W., and C. C. Shelby. *Revolt of the Pueblo Indians of New Mexico and Otermin's Attempted Reconquest, 1680–1682*. Albuquerque: University of New Mexico Press, 1945.

Hewett, Edgar L., and Bertha Dutton. *The Pueblo Indian World*. Santa Fe: School of American Research, 1945.

Hungry Wolf, Beverly. *The Ways of My Grandmothers*. New York: William Morrow, 1980.

Jenkins, Myra Ellen. *Taos Pueblo and Its Neighbors, 1540–1847*. New Mexico Historical Review XLI:2, 1966.

Kelly, Lawrence C. *The Assault on Assimilation: John Collier and the Origins of Indian Policy Reform*. Albuquerque: University of New Mexico Press, 1983.

La Barre, Weston. *The Peyote Cult*. New York: Schocken Books, 1975.

Luhan, Mabel Dodge. *Winter in Taos*. Denver: Sage Books, 1935.

McNierney, Michael, ed. *Taos 1847: The Revolt in Contemporary Accounts*. Boulder, Col.: Johnson Publishing Company, 1980.

McNitt, Frank. *Navajo Wars*. Albuquerque: University of New Mexico Press, 1972.

Mails, Thomas E. *The Pueblo Indians* (two vols.). New York: Doubleday, 1981.

————. *Sundancing at Rosebud and Pine Ridge*. Lake Mills, Iowa: Center for Western Studies, 1978.

Marriott, Alice, and Carol K. Rachlin. *American Indian Mythology*. New York: Thomas Y. Crowell, 1968.

Martineau, La Van. *The Rocks Begin to Speak*. Las Vegas, Nev.: H & R Printing, 1968.

Meinig, D. W. *Southwest: Three Peoples in Geographical Change 1600–1970*. New York: Oxford University Press, 1971.

Miller, Merton Leland. *A Preliminary Study of the Pueblo of Taos, New Mexico*. Chicago: University of Chicago Press, 1898.

Momaday, N. Scott. *House Made of Dawn*. New York: Harper & Row, 1968.

————. *The Way to Rainy Mountain*. Albuquerque: University of New Mexico Press, 1969.

Morrill, Claire. *A Taos Mosaic: Portrait of a New Mexico Village*. Albuquerque: University of New Mexico Press, 1973.

Nabokov, Peter. *Indian Running*. New York: Capra, 1981.

————, ed. *Native American Testimony*. New York: Thomas Y. Crowell, 1978.

Neihard, John G. (Transcription). *Black Elk Speaks: Being the Life Story of a Holy Man of the Oglala Sioux*. Lincoln: University of Nebraska Press, 1961.

New Mexico: A Guide to the Colorful State. Compiled by workers of the Writers' Program of the Works Progress Administration, Coronado Cuarto Centennial Commission. New York: American Guide Series, Hastings House, 1940.

Olson, James S., and Raymond Wilson. *Native Americans in the Twentieth Century*. Urbana: University of Illinois Press, 1984.

Ortiz, Alfonso, ed. *New Perspectives on the Pueblos*. Albuquerque: School of American Research, University of New Mexico, 1972.

————. *The Tewa World: Space, Time, and Being in a Pueblo Society*. Chicago and London: University of Chicago Press, 1969.

Parsons, Elsie Clews. *Pueblo Indian Religion* (two vols.). Chicago: University of Chicago Press, 1939.

————. *Taos Pueblo*. Menasha, Wis.: George Banta, 1936.

————. *Taos Tales*. New York: Kraus Reprint Company, 1969.

Reno, Philip. *Taos Pueblo*. Chicago: Swallow Press, 1972.

Sando, Joe S. *The Pueblo Indians*. San Francisco: Indian Historian Press, 1976.

Scholes, France V. *Troublous Times in New Mexico, 1659–1670*. Albuquerque: University of New Mexico Press, 1942.

Silko, Leslie Marmon. *Storyteller*. New York: Seaver Books, 1981.

Spicer, Edward H. *Cycles of Conquest*. Tucson: University of Arizona Press, 1962.

Spinden, Herbert J. *Songs of the Tewa*. Santa Fe: Sunstone Press, 1976.

Tyler, Hamilton A. *Pueblo Gods and Myths*. Norman: University of Oklahoma, 1964.

Underhill, Ruth. *Workaday Life of the Pueblos*. Washington, D.C.: United States Information Service, n.d.

Waters, Frank. *Book of the Hopi*. New York: Viking, 1963.

————. *The Man Who Killed the Deer*. Denver: Sage Books, 1942.

————. *Masked Gods: Navajo and Pueblo Ceremonials*. Albuquerque: University of New Mexico Press, 1950.

————. *Pumpkin Seed Point*. Chicago: Sage Books, 1969.

Witt, Shirley Hill, and Stan Steiner, eds. *The Way: An Anthology of American Indian Literature*. New York: Alfred A. Knopf, 1972.

Wood, Nancy. *Hollering Sun*. New York: Simon & Schuster, 1972.

————. *The Man Who Gave Thunder to the Earth*. New York: Doubleday, 1976.

————. *Many Winters*. New York: Doubleday, 1974.

————. *War Cry on a Prayer Feather*. New York: Doubleday, 1979.

————. *When Buffalo Free the Mountains*. New York: Doubleday, 1981.

Zinn, Howard. *A People's History of the United States*. New York: Harper & Row, 1980.

A NOTE ABOUT THE AUTHOR

Nancy Wood, photographer, poet, and novelist, was born in 1936
in Trenton, New Jersey. Her close association with Taos Pueblo
led to the publication of two volumes of poetry on the Pueblo,
Many Winters and *Hollering Sun*, as well as a novel, *The Man Who
Gave Thunder to the Earth*. Her third volume of poetry, *War Cry on a
Prayer Feather*, was set to music. She is also the author of many
photography books, including *The Grass Roots People*. In 1987,
Nancy Wood was awarded a Literary Fellowship from the
National Endowment for the Arts. She lives in Taos, where she
is at work on a new novel.

A NOTE ON THE TYPE

This book was set in Novarese, created by the European
designer, Aldo Novarese, well known for such typefaces as
Eurostile, Egizio, Torino and Nova Augustea.

   Novarese's distinctive, classic style is derived from its graceful
curves and finely chiseled serifs. The contrast between its thick
and thin strokes is noticeable but not extreme, giving the text a
sparkle without sacrificing readability.

Composed by The Sarabande Press, New York, New York,
Stonetone reproductions and printing by Rapoport Printing
Corporation, New York, New York. Bound by A. Horowitz, Fairfield,
New Jersey.

Map by Claudia Carlson

Designed by Virginia Tan